D1038848

PLANTS IN THE GETTY'S CENTRAL GARDEN

JIM DUGGAN

PLANTS IN THE GETTY'S CENTRAL GARDEN

Garden photography by Becky Cohen
with additional photography by Jim Duggan
Foreword by Robert Irwin

The J. Paul Getty Museum, Los Angeles

DEDICATION

To Bob Irwin, with thanks for sharing his garden with me; to Gary Byrnes, for giving me my first nursery; to Mark Owens, for inviting me to my present nursery; to the Getty Center and the Getty's Grounds Department, for their ongoing support and encouragement; to the Central Garden crew, who tend the garden so well every day; and to the Aloha spirit of Silver Cloud Ranch, for providing the peace and quiet in which this book was written.

© 2003 J. Paul Getty Trust

Getty Publications
1200 Getty Center Drive
Suite 500
Los Angeles, California 90049-1682
www.getty.edu

Christopher Hudson, Publisher
Mark Greenberg, Editor in Chief

John Harris, Editor
Markus Brilling, Designer
Suzanne Watson, Production Coordinator
Arthur C. Gibson, Botanical Consultant

Typography by Diane Franco
Map illustration by Dusty Deyo
Color separations by Professional Graphics Inc., Rockford, Illinois
Printed by Tien Wah Press, Singapore

Library of Congress Cataloging-in-Publication Data

Duggan, Jim.
  Plants in the Getty's central garden / Jim Duggan ;
garden photography by Becky Cohen ;
with additional photography by Jim Duggan ; foreword by Robert Irwin.

      p. cm.

Includes bibliographical references and index.
ISBN 0-89236-714-8 (pbk.)
1. Getty Center Gardens (Los Angeles, Calif.) 2. Gardens--California--Los Angeles.
 3. Plants, Ornamental--California--Los Angeles. 4. Irwin, Robert, 1928- I. Cohen, Becky.
II. Title.

SB466.U7G483 2004
635.9'09794'94--dc21

2003008169

CONTENTS

EVER   EVER
PRESENT   CHANGING
NEVER   NEVER
TWICE THE SAME   LESS THAN WHOLE

When I began work on the Getty's Central Garden, I thought in time I would deliver a complete planting plan that the Getty could simply implement. But a garden doesn't lend itself to such a static solution . . . and it taught me again about the meaning of process, something I thought I already knew.

There is nothing more phenomenological than a garden . . . and for an artist who has come to regard the aesthetics of individual perception as the universal subject of art, the Getty garden was a new awakening. Gardening frustrates all of our conventional ideas . . . and defies all of our desires to order and to plan, to transcend our circumstances by relying on the myths of fixed concepts. It seems to me that there is no better place to undertake an extended inquiry into the rhyme and reason for "art in public places," and no better opportunity to question the true nature of our being in the world.

Gardening requires the ultimate hands-on, everyday "attending" . . . a process, where we optimistically set in motion our desires for how we want things to be . . . and in turn discover how things actually are . . . and then we learn to work at keeping them in play.

Working in the garden with Jim Duggan has been a true collaboration . . . we have enjoyed together the discoveries and pleasures of a shared authorship in the creation of what is and always will be a work in progress.

Robert Irwin

GARDENING THE GETTY: THREE ESSAYS

THROUGH AN ARTIST'S EYE

The imposing J. Paul Getty Center in Los Angeles is a must-see destination for local and world travelers alike. Set on a mountain perch, the pristine geometry of the travertine-clad buildings attracts thousands every day to view the unique architecture and art collection. Secreted in the center of all this activity is a living sculpture, made in the form of a garden, offering a counterpoint to the overall Getty experience. Artist Robert Irwin has created this sculpture by presenting a series of outdoor experiences with changing levels of engagement. Irwin attempts to take the visitor from the grand mountaintop views into a garden of ever-increasing sensory involvement, where the discovery of a single flower may offer a uniquely memorable encounter.

Typical of Irwin's art, there are no signposts telling us how to see or what to expect. Instead, like a Siren's call, the garden entices us away from the white architectural vistas. The first glimpse for many visitors is the overlook at the top of the garden. From here Irwin's living sculpture, in lush greenery, attracts the viewer like a magnet.

Often coupled with this initial view of the garden is the remembered controversy surrounding its development. Television shows and magazine articles chronicled a "clash of wills" in the planning process. The Getty Trust chose to intervene in architect Richard Meier's design for the future garden space. In their desire to introduce a different, more intimate element, the Trust invited Bob Irwin, an artist born and raised in Los Angeles, to submit a proposal for the garden. Irwin is known for his ability to intimately engage a wide range of viewers and awaken in them their own perceptual processes. His challenge was to respond to the strong geometry of the architecture and blend it with the requirements that a garden presents.

Early on, critics and skeptics were uncomfortable with Irwin's crossing of boundaries and his weaving together of traditionally distinct definitions. Meier saw this intervention as a disruption in the clarity of his architectural ambition. Landscape architects and garden designers saw it as an invasion of their territory. How could an artist, and a nongardener at that, ever expect to effectively lay out the structural bones and plan the horticultural intricacies of a living garden? And during the opening months the gardening press certainly felt vindicated by Irwin's lack of plant knowledge, resulting, they said, in the creation of an inappropriate landscape and the choice of inappropriate plant materials. His response was a single word: Patience.

Irwin approached landscape design through the eyes of an artist. Confronted by the staggering potential in nature's variety, he began to explore the full range of this new palette, and I was fortunate enough to be chosen to help Bob in this huge endeavor. Irwin and I made countless nursery visits up and down the West Coast. We took the time to seek out the smaller nursery/gardens of true plant enthusiasts. There his own enthusiasm and obvious pleasure were contagious. It was enlightening for me to observe Irwin as he searched for plant material with his artist's eye.

Primary to Irwin's way of seeing is his unique connection to the elements of perception. Instead of seeing in terms of species and cultivars, he sees in terms of pure form and structure. Light, space, and color for him are tactile; each has a distinct visual density. Textures, patterns, and surfaces activate color into pure energy. These fundamental perceptions act as the unifying ground for all his inquiries and practices, making it possible for him to cross over and explore other disciplines. Irwin always adds one essential factor to the artistic equation: Each time he must start at the beginning, putting himself on a radical learning curve to acquire the particulars necessary to practice his art.

Irwin studied his subject deeply, from countless angles. He gathered a team of specialists to cover areas where his own expertise was lacking. As with his other art projects, there was an overriding dedication to detail. For example, to give flesh to his early thoughts and to bridge the differences in our backgrounds, he cut up stacks of garden books to create large collages. Each collage exhibited the various qualities of color, leaf, and texture for each section of the garden. These pictures acted to ground our dialogue. While it is a huge leap from a collage to a real garden, there was something unique here, because the concept began at an artistic, painterly level. In this detailed way Irwin educated himself, carefully engaging each collaborator he would need for every facet of his project.

The flowering of Irwin's sculpture will inevitably have a life of its own as plants change size and appearance with each season. Some will flourish and others will unexpectedly perish. It takes a gardener's eye to see the changes and a gardener's skill to deal with the surprises. (As I often tell visitors at the Getty, "I am the plant side of Bob Irwin.") At my nursery he constantly asked—and still asks—"What about this plant, where does it go from here?" It's been my job to see for him, to picture for him the full evolution of each plant. He needs to know its size, color, and leaf character, even how it will look when it's dying away. Sometimes I must temper his unbridled enthusiasm with a cool dose of reality. Yet on the occasions when he has had a strong feeling for a plant that might be marginal, we've simply brought it to my nursery garden (which is similar to the Getty's eco-setting) and grown it to see what would happen. This de facto collaboration between artist and gardener has made for a number of happy discoveries. The garden is filled with them.

While admiring a section of the garden, a visitor remarked to her companion that she would return home and plant her garden "Getty-like." She isn't alone: Irwin's creation is helping to carve out new territory in California's gardening world. Taking a cue from Irwin's living sculpture, gardeners may try some of his painterly combinations themselves; emboldened, they too may drop an orange-colored sedge (*Carex testacea*) into a group of gray-leaved plants. Finding what Irwin calls the "kicker" color an exciting expansion of current garden theory, amateur gardeners may decide to nestle purple-flowered heliotrope next to the chartreuse leaves of *Campanula* 'Dickson's Gold'. Not fearing diversity, some may seek out new plants, like the lusciously bold *Geranium maderense*, the largest of the true geraniums, and find a place for it in their own garden. After seeing the mint-green flowered hellebores (Lenten roses), they will ask their garden center to carry these old-fashioned plants. The gardeners of Southern California may even go so far as to use deciduous plants to create striking yet subtle effects in wintertime.

Robert Irwin's presentation—his sculpture in the form of a garden—adds a new page to Southern California's garden history. His artist's approach to gardening will inevitably influence many who know nothing at all about modern art. Change is in the air, this garden tells us. Listen. And—most of all—look.

A GARDENER MEETS AN ARTIST

Gardening has become a very powerful force in my life. It began simply enough with a few pots of marigold and alyssum filling a small clearing outside my kitchen window. This small start at appreciating Mother Nature's intricate and ever-changing mosaic quickly blossomed into a nearly addictive passion. I purchased more plants, while the clearing outside the kitchen grew to envelop the entire front yard. At the time I was making my living as a ceramic tile contractor. During the week I floated mortar beds and fashioned colorful designs from fired clay. On my days off I could always be found in my garden. Rather than going to the beach or the park to play, I would spend my day off weeding and raking. This added "work" brought a joy and satisfaction that my non-gardener friends found difficult to understand. There is indeed a lot of work involved in tending a garden, but it is also a meditation that calms and refreshes the spirit. Seeing a small seed transform into a brilliant flower, collecting flowers for the vase, taking in their fragrance—all are part of a gardener's stimulating world.

This refreshing work changed my life's direction. The kitchen garden grew into a small retail nursery. I also began a modest garden design and consultation service and a specialized mail-order business featuring South African bulbs. My nursery life developed in stages while I continued to set tile to make ends meet. Many days I began watering at the crack of dawn and then loaded my truck with tools for a full day of setting tile.

My first nursery was an integral part of an early design project. A friend was developing an eleven-acre parcel in Vista, California, into a health-care facility. Sensing the rehabilitative effect that gardening offers, I surrounded the new project with beautiful gardens. Rare trees, grown from seed, formed an arboretum. An inveterate plant collector, I blanketed the site with a wide array of flowering plants. Unfortunately, financial difficulties brought an ownership change, and my tiling tools were again loaded into my truck.

Although I lost this garden, the experience left me substantially wiser in the art of garden development. I moved the nursery with its collection of rare plants to the coastal Southern California community of Encinitas. Here I started a small retail nursery, Encinitas Gardens, and continued my effort to leave tile work behind. I specialized in plants adapted to a Mediterranean climate, often rare and unusual ones. One frequent customer was searching for new Australian plants for his own garden. This client, Lane Goodkind, also worked with the landscape architecture firm of Spurlock

Poirier. Once, while I added up his order, he began to talk about a project he was working on, the new Getty Museum being constructed in Los Angeles. Later, after we became friends, Lane related that it was a very unusual project in that the lead designer was neither a landscape architect nor a gardener but an artist, a painter and sculptor. On one occasion, Goodkind commented that the artist had chosen a grass for the new garden, a rather common and weedy pennisetum, and everyone was trying to steer him in another direction. We both laughed at the artist's apparent lack of knowledge in picking this weedy grass.

This was near the end of 1995. Over the next few months I learned more about this amazing new museum and garden. Spurlock Poirier, the landscape architects, were continually perplexed by the artist's choices of plant materials. On one visit Lane offered a proposition. The artist, Robert Irwin, had put together a list of plant materials gleaned from books and visits to nurseries. Showing me the list, Lane asked if I could obtain samples of the plants and grow them here at my nursery so that Irwin and the landscape architects could view their growth over a period of time. I had extra space and certainly could use the money, so I prepared a proposal for collecting and maintaining the plants for a period of six months. Spurlock accepted the proposal, and I started my first project for the Getty.

The plant list was quite large, several hundred specimens, and I was to collect two of each, a task akin to filling Noah's Ark. I did the best I could, but many of the plants had little to do with Southern California, as the books Irwin had drawn from were based on other areas of the country. Here began a magical turn of fate. Bob Irwin, Lane Goodkind, and other plant designers from Spurlock Poirier came to my nursery every few weeks to begin work with the growing collection of plants. At first I stayed in the background, observing the interaction between Irwin and the designers. They played with various combinations, assembling different groupings on my rear patio. During his visits Irwin began to walk around my nursery, always being inquisitive. Apparently he liked what he saw: more and more he turned to me for information. "What about this plant, where does it go from here?" was his most commonly asked question. Irwin was searching for plants that fit his artistic vision. Although I didn't yet understand that vision, we clearly found common ground in the plant-selection process. I admired his adventuresome palette, and he admired many of the plants I had stocked in my retail nursery.

Irwin and I found further common ground in another area. On hearing of my new role in collecting plants for Irwin, a friend showed me an article she had saved from the *New Yorker*. As a dance teacher she had enjoyed reading of this artist who was also a dancer. In the piece the artist—Bob Irwin himself—recounted his favorite dance steps. My friend and I were swing dancers and had even taught together some time back. What a surprise it was to learn that Irwin and I shared this passion. As dancers we find the dynamic partnering of the jitterbug and lindy to be a significant force in our lives. Dancing is like a drug, something we both need on a regular basis. In his youth Irwin was a champion lindy dancer; he still talks of a unique shoulder twist he employed when attempting to take flight on the dance floor. In a later generation I constantly wore holes in my jazz oxfords while one-stepping. Thus our new friendship found its footing in the lively beat of swing music. This bond made it easier for me to step out of the background. Irwin's frequent visits brought us closer together as we played off each other's enthusiasms and expertise. He needed advice on plants, while I began to learn more about the intricacies of color and form that direct his way of seeing.

Armed with Bob's list I collected as many plants as possible from Southern California sources, but I soon began to realize that I would have to go out of the area. I made this suggestion to Bob, and he quickly responded that I would need to submit a written proposal that outlined this plant search. During the last ten to fifteen years I had used my spring vacation to visit nurseries, botanical gardens, and arboretums throughout California, and I really knew what was out there. I submitted my proposal.

And so, to my great delight, in the summer of 1996 I set off on a plant lover's dream. I rented a fifteen-foot truck, built shelves at different heights, and proceeded to visit all of my favorite sources scattered around the state. Irwin's instructions were simple: to fill the holes in his list and—how lucky can you get?—to bring back anything that I thought was interesting. The plant quest proved different on many levels from my earlier spring trips. Of course, the size of the truck and the funds in my wallet allowed me to collect much more than on any previous venture. But something else was different, though I didn't realize it at first. I was beginning to look at plants in a new way and find them valuable for new reasons. Rare shrubs from Australia and South Africa that fit my Mediterranean climate theme still caught my eye, yet somehow—imperceptibly at first—I began to notice plants with certain leaf textures and surprising flower juxtapositions. During Irwin's visits to my nursery a collaboration and an education had begun that would transform my view of nature's intricate patterns.

The most surprising and delightful aspect of Irwin's art is this taking of the traditional view of the world and subliminally redirecting the eye to explore and experience other levels of perception. At first you might be taken aback, caught off guard perhaps, and dismiss or even laugh at what you see. When Lane first mentioned the common and weedy grass that Irwin had admired, I laughed and dismissed the idea as amateurish. But it wasn't that particular grass which was important to Irwin; it was a certain look and feel that he sought. And the grass that he did choose, after reviewing countless candidates, turned out to be exactly right for his purposes.

Something similar happened later on, when it came time to choose the trees that were to line the stream that zigzags down the Central Garden. Irwin was looking for a tree "with stature" that would do well in Southern California. He visited many nurseries and asked advice from some of the best people in the business. This led him to look at the London plane tree. Everyone was recommending the variety 'Bloodgood' as the best grower and the most disease-resistant. Irwin traveled to Oregon to personally pick and tag the 'Bloodgoods' for the project. He was about to sign a contract when he crossed paths with Barrie Coate, a noted plantsman from Santa Cruz. Coate was adamant that what Irwin wanted was the variety 'Yarwood', not 'Bloodgood'. In this he differed from everyone else Irwin had talked to. But there was something about Barrie Coate that inspired confidence, and so Irwin traveled to Santa Cruz and spent the day with Coate to find out why he felt as he did. Convinced, Irwin traveled back to Oregon and changed his order to 'Yarwood', getting the last ones available. In due course the trees arrived in Southern California. The following spring Irwin viewed the new additions to the garden. There was a large block of 'Bloodgoods' next to the 'Yarwoods'. The 'Bloodgoods' were struggling, while the 'Yarwoods' were in lush condition. Irwin had done his homework. He didn't know a lot about trees when he started, but by always asking, looking, and listening, he educated himself. And in the end the 'Yarwood' is a great tree "with stature" for the Central Garden.

After two weeks on the road I returned home with a truckload of new plant material for Irwin to review. We were both excited by the numerous and varied selections laid out in the nursery parking lot. Again he asked, "Where does this plant go from here?" "How big does it get?" "Do the leaves retain a particular sheen or coloration?" "Would this plant succeed in sun or shade?" Our collaboration deepened and expanded as we shared comments and perceptions. Later, when he continued the selection process with Spurlock Poirier, Irwin invited my opinion more often. Something clicked between us, allowing the design to get closer to the artistic direction he sought. Spurlock Poirier was having a difficult time interpreting Irwin's plant ideas, and they quickly noticed that I was able to offer more solutions.

Incredibly, fate stepped forward when, in the fall of 1996, Andy Spurlock asked me if I would like to try my hand at developing the plant design with Irwin. It took my breath away. I was struggling to advance my retail nursery, setting tile to pay for new plants and potting soil, and now this immense opportunity was placed before me. I was to work closely with Irwin to prepare the plant composition for the future garden. My part-time job now emerged from the background to become my full-time job: to study Irwin and decipher his unusual and artistic view of gardening. We initiated a series of meetings and exploratory trips to nurseries and gardens so that I could better understand what moved him to select a particular plant. Irwin's approach would prove to be unlike anything I had thus far encountered.

One key difference was, and is, that Irwin cares little if a plant is rare or common; he focuses instead on how a plant can add to his overall artistic aesthetic. (His choice of grass demonstrated this.) If I were to be successful in interpreting Irwin's art with plants, it was obvious that I would need to learn more about his unique way of perceiving them in terms of form and structure. And so our collaboration began to move back and forth between our individual areas of expertise. Irwin, a nongardener, sought plant knowledge from me, while I sought his knowledge of the essential elements of perception.

I often surprised Bob with elaborate Latin plant names; he in turn mystified me with technical descriptions of color. For example, Irwin sought a red accent for an area in the garden, and it needed to be a red of unadulterated hue. Traveling through a nursery we would encounter twenty different plants with red flowers, and Irwin would proceed to dissect each one into its hue, value, and intensity. Technically, red is a very dominant color, affecting its neighbors while being nearly untouched by them. A true red—one unmixed with other colors, one of full hue—offered the maximum expression for the garden. It should be neither overly dark—that is, lower in value, with more black added—nor should it be infused with white, which gives it a washed-out value. A powerful red, one with the greatest intensity (or saturation) and having the highest percentage of pure hue, was the goal we sought. When a suitable color was found, regardless of the genus it represented, we made every effort to bring it into the design.

Combined with this technical approach to color is Irwin's grasp of texture and form as they embody nature's spontaneous weaving together of leaves and flowers. A controlling hand is absent, yet no mistakes are found; everything fits so well together.

For Irwin, this sensual weaving together is the ultimate success in a garden. In my garden a large specimen of *Pelargonium* 'Irvine', with its dark green leaves and surprising orange-tinted flowers, exceeds its own beauty and finds further glory when the purple-pink flowers of a nearby ivy geranium twine through the surrounding leaves. Irwin constantly reminds us that the specimen is often enhanced when unexpectedly woven in with its neighbors. The Getty garden was not to be a collection of individually presented plants but rather a garden of interwoven textures and colors.

I now had a new mission: to find painterly colors and strive for a tapestry effect in presentation. Along with constant nursery and garden explorations I also interviewed respected garden designers and growers who would share gems of knowledge gleaned from their experience. For true geraniums I met with Robin Parer, the delightful Marin County grower. I always asked for personal favorites and for what she thought would do well in Southern California. I purchased Robin's favorites and added them to the growing collection at my nursery. A standout performer would be the *Geranium* 'Ann Folkard' with its large, golden-green leaves and incredible purple flowers on long, intertwining runners: perfect for a bright area of the garden. Robin's garden has an area she calls her bruised and battered border, and from this I chose several exciting combinations. I particularly liked the golden-leaved creeping moneywort (*Lysimachia nummularia* 'Aurea'), with black mondo grass as an accent. Both plants came to my nursery and found their way into the new garden design.

For a true garden feeling it was essential to find roses to incorporate into the composition. I met with the plant breeder Tom Carruth and secured a list of his favorites. He generously gave me a bag of freshly dug bare root varieties to try, including a new unnamed climber. In answer to my quest for a true red rose, he added three or four potential candidates. Continuing the Noah's Ark approach, I purchased two each of the roses Carruth recommended and grew them at my nursery. There were several winners in this group, especially the extravagantly rich red 'Trumpeter' rose, a wonderful two-and-a-half-foot bush, nearly everblooming, with remarkably good, clean foliage. Surprisingly few of my rose-growing friends knew this rose, an apparently older introduction that I could not find in any current catalogue. 'Trumpeter' is a great plant, a really red rose that would soon find a permanent home in Irwin's garden.

From each interview, each visit to a garden, an idea would come that added a thread to our garden tapestry. While chatting with Judy Wigand in her flower-filled garden nursery I admired the engagingly colored 'Black Beauty' heliotrope. Irwin sought plants with dark foliage for part of his design, and this old garden favorite seemed perfect. It can be short-lived, and I was reticent to use it, but Judy's own plant had flourished for several years, and so her success secured a place for 'Black Beauty' in the garden.

I had a similar experience walking through the garden of Chris Rosmini, the renowned garden designer in Los Angeles. Under the canopy of an exceptional stand of aged pines Chris had planted the remarkable combination of purple-leaved *Cercis* 'Forest Pansy' and the golden *Robinia pseudoacacia* 'Frisia'. From the literature I understood that this golden honey locust should not be successful so far south, but there it was, standing before me in perfect form and sparkling color. This encounter reinforced my own perception that although a particular plant is thought to be unsuccessful in a particular area, there can be microclimates in that area where the plant will succeed.

Broadening the acceptable palette of plants for Southern California was one of our goals for the new garden, and I tried to offer Irwin a broad spectrum of choices with which he could could create his living sculpture. He and I share an affection for variety, and nature's boundless palette continually supplies new material for us to try. Irwin uses plants sculpturally to convey common themes in new ways and to present original concepts.

One of these concepts that even I found a bit too odd upon first hearing it was Irwin's scheme for a winter garden. Here in Southern California the word deciduous is absent from most landscape design theory, and dormancy is an alien idea. Without winter's chill, gardeners here focus on evergreen shrubs and perennials, as well as plants that flower year-round. Although born and raised in Los Angeles, Irwin travels extensively, and he came to the conclusion that winter's features could be emphasized. In early discussions he continually pressed for a more open, much quieter, perhaps even stark look for the garden in winter. Virtually everyone, including me, felt that this was at best unwise, if not downright crazy. We could have color year-round in our climate; why not take advantage of that wonderful fact? But Irwin was persistent. His thinking was that both of our major stands of trees—London plane and crape myrtle— are deciduous, and our major stands of *Muhlenbergia* grass are cut back for the winter. Why not consider the added complexity of a winter season? He continually asked me to locate plants with interesting bark and branch structure that, when bare, would heighten winter's effect. Plants with berries, on bare stems too, were highly sought after. He even intended to leave the ground bare in areas of the garden. We went to great pains to create a soil that was dark in color, like Iowa loam, so unlike our pale, even whitish soils. Irwin's concept for a winter garden was the unique insight of a nongardener for whom everything is seen as a part of the picture.

Even in our California sunshine, winter feels different. The days are shorter, curtailing the outdoor experience. Temperatures drop, and I find I wear long pants and a sweatshirt instead of the usual shorts and T-shirt. The light of the sky itself changes, producing softer exposures. For plant health, it's a good time to prune back shrubs and divide favorite perennials. At the Getty we further amplified the effect by adding plants whose leaves are absent, exposing their bare branches. We used the shrub form of the red and yellow twig dogwoods *Cornus stolonifera* 'Isanti' and 'Flaverimea', with the colorfully barked willows *Salix* 'Flame' and *S. irrorata* 'Blue-Stem Willow'. These elicit an incredible response; everyone wants to know what they are. We continued to use them as winter annuals, digging them in early spring and placing them back in pots. They spend the summer at the nursery and then are returned to the garden in the fall (the reverse of bringing in tender plants for the winter). I really don't believe many gardeners here would have tried this; it had to be someone outside of the arena.

Irwin is stirred by the innate structure of plants. His eye is enamored of the play of branch and leaf; he often finds the flower a secondary experience. He proposed the use of ornamental grasses, possibly to be displayed in pots set around the garden. Together we sought out the "Pied Piper" of grasses, John Greenlee, at his nursery in Pomona. Greenlee generously shared favorite varieties with us, including a few new but unidentified introductions. In all we amassed some forty-five different grasses that I brought to my nursery to be grown and evaluated. Every few months we catalogued the changes in structure of each candidate, trying to determine the best moment for its display. Irwin would find interest in the angle of a stem, the play of light through crossing leaves, the dance of wind amidst feathery seed heads. Many of the grasses are winter dormant, becoming erect clumps of tan dry stalks. Invariably this somnolent display of structure alone is what most attracts Irwin's eye. Gardeners in colder climates value this effect, with winter's snow and ice accenting the dormant stems. Here in evergreen Southern California, many gardeners deliberately cut the faded stalks to the ground. Irwin, though, seeks to feature this structural effect in winter, letting it add to the quietness of the period.

While we were touring nurseries and gardens, this predilection to see structure and visual character often elicited a classic response from Irwin. He would single out one specimen from a block of identical cousins and rhapsodize over the fascinating combination of leaf color and structure of that particular plant. And then I would have to tell him, "Bob, that plant is sick and dying." I sometimes found it humorous that his vision could be so far removed from the common perception of most gardeners.

One day in the Central Garden Bob asked about the large planting of *Kalanchoe pumila* that surrounds his azalea pool. This gray-leaved plant can become infused with a reddish glow in winter. The red coloring, seen in many kinds of plants, is the result of the chemical pigment anthocyanin. Cooler temperatures or plant stress will increase the amount of this pigment. Irwin noticed that a new section of this kalanchoe planted in another area of the garden was showing a lot of red, while the large planting in question was not. I explained that the reddish plants were newly planted and had come from a part of the nursery where care was minimal. They were indeed stressed by receiving less fertilizer and water and therefore had redder coloring. Irwin responded, "Well then, stress those plants! Give them a little loving stress!" Not for the first time I found myself thinking: Here is a gardener with a different approach.

A great variety of plants had now been gathered, and Irwin and I began assembling various combinations. Irwin continually demonstrated his artistic skill. He introduced me to the concept of using "kicker" colors, which activate the palette and put colors in motion. In an area of skillfully arranged gray-toned plants that showed great promise together, Irwin would drop in an orange or yellow flower. The combination now would come to life, the grays reading much stronger. This technique works in many directions, raising or lowering the level of visual activity, in one use emboldening the combination, in another softening the overall effect.

After completing a grouping of plants, finding good direction and a measure of success in each, we would repeat the process, trying out more plants from our growing collection. I then proceeded to set the design down on paper, trying to capture the best groupings for the architectural plan.

Up until this point I had not visited the project site. Hours had been spent poring over the architectural drawings, studying elevations and noting structural items such as footing and irrigation layout, but as yet I could only imagine the physical size of the project. Although I am a building contractor, I was unprepared for the complexity of the Getty experience. It was late fall 1996, rain had fallen the night before, and my white tennis shoes would soon be soiled, I thought, as I pulled into the entrance of the Getty Center.

First there was a multilevel parking structure that, except for the upper floor, was buried in the ground. The excavation alone for this building astonished me. To reach the museum buildings, perched on a hilltop, a small tram traveled up an undulating slope. On arrival I was overwhelmed by the scope of the project as numerous giant cranes carried materials to hundreds of construction workers. After checking in at security I was required to don a hard hat and safety vest displaying an appropriate badge. I then traversed vast and confusing corridors to reach the future garden area. There were more cranes, tractors, scaffolding, and workers everywhere. Daunted by the activity level within, I walked around the perimeter of the area. The space was considerably more expansive than I had anticipated. The future Stream Garden was completely covered with machinery, piles of dirt, and workmen heading in all directions; at least the Bowl Garden was taking on its rounded form. The floor of the future azalea pool was in place, and workmen were building elaborate, maze-like forms. Lying everywhere were huge plates of curved steel. Some had been bolted onto large footings to become expansive arcs radiating from the central pool. Standing at the southern edge of this space, I was left breathless by its monumental scale.

My inaugural visit to the Getty swept me into a fast-running stream. It had been in design and construction for nearly a decade, and now there were whispers of deadlines. I set my own, unofficial deadline to present a completed design for early winter. In concert with this future design Irwin thought of another role for me to play. Clearly the numerous varieties of plants that I had brought to his attention would not be readily available from local nurseries. Obtaining the material for planting in timely fashion required a plan in itself. Irwin saw my nursery as the ideal solution. If I could expand the growing area at my nursery we could collect and store plant material when it became available. The plants not available in sufficient quantity needed to be propagated and grown to planting size. So I cleared a new field, rolled out ground cloth, installed new irrigation and timers, and ordered small starter plants. This newly expanded growing area was soon bustling with activity and was beginning to give us a feeling of what the future Getty garden would be. Here were the actual plants, conveniently at hand, allowing us to update our groupings continually.

Seeing the plants in my growing area, Irwin was assured that we were on the right track. But the successful execution of his plan over an extended period was going to prove challenging. He knew this from experience. In at least one of his previous art and garden pieces the installation had been successful but the after-care proved disastrous. Observing the care I gave not only to the plants but also to the planting process, Bob now invited me to explore yet another role and take part in the planting and care of his garden. This mirrors a view I have often championed in my role as a retail nurseryman. I preach to my clients that a garden needs a gardener—a down-on-your-knees gardener—a simple proposition that is frequently overlooked. Customers obtain a garden plan, hire a landscape contractor to install irrigation, plant the site, and then fail to follow through with the real care a garden requires. Knowing this, many designers limit the choice of plants to those that require little attention. I define this as landscaping, which is different from gardening in that it does not require ongoing involvement. Most clients seek to enhance the value of their home with a garden, as they would with a new kitchen design or an added entertainment center; they do not want to become gardeners. Those who enter into the garden world, though, find it necessary and enjoyable to spend much more time with their plants. A successful garden requires this added attention.

Irwin took my views on garden care to heart. The Getty garden needed—and will always need—an active, hands-on gardener. My role with the garden would deepen as I followed and directed its growth after the initial installation.

One of the most important facets that I had to address was the health and vitality of the soil. For an artist like Bob the soil is a design element, and Irwin sought a rich, dark color. My focus was different: to offer the plants the best possible soil to grow in. Good drainage is essential, and so we searched for a source of sandy loam, admittedly rare in Southern California. The dark color that Irwin was pushing for doesn't really exist here. We added black scoria rock, a volcanic material, that would darken the color as well as benefit drainage and promote root development with its sharp-edged particles. To supply the soil with life I suggested the addition of worm castings, which are also very dark. This valuable product, the result of worms digesting organic matter, adds an increased level of life to the soil structure. The final combination produces a richly colored combination with a lively soil structure—a perfect canvas for Irwin to work on.

During the installation of the garden in the winter of 1997, Southern California and the world received an onslaught of El Niño weather. The amount of rain and wind we endured while planting the garden was unbelievable. On more than one occasion the wind blew so hard that newly planted shrubs were literally pulled out of the ground. Rain came in such torrents that soil and worm castings, unprotected by binding roots and leaf cover, suffered damaging erosion. On the west side of the Bowl, castings had been applied, while on the east side, due to the severe weather, it was decided to wait until spring. Somehow I was not informed of this decision and believed that all of the castings were in place. During the first months after planting I was continually perplexed by the uneven growth patterns in the Bowl. Active, even lush growth was taking place on the west side, while the east side seemed to languish. Problems with the irrigation system forced us to water some areas by hand, so I directed that careful watering and additional fertilizers be applied, yet the pattern continued. In passing, one of the garden crew mentioned the absence of the castings on the east side. Buzzers and bells immediately went off in my head. Everything else was the same: the soil, the plants, the weather; only the castings were different. We immediately applied a one-inch layer of worm castings to the east side and in short order the growth there picked up and soon rivaled that on the west side.

It was a challenging time to plant a new garden, with El Niño roaring in the background, but the severest challenge was the constraint of time. Construction continued at a feverish pitch, with the opening date set for December 1997. It was nearing the end of October when I brought the first plants to the garden: four boxed specimens of *Euphorbia cotinifolia*, the copper tree. Not a single plant was in the ground, and the opening was less than eight weeks away. Construction on the various buildings had held up our start of the Stream Garden; the Bowl Garden was far from finished, as the soil mix had only recently been installed. Cranes hoisted the four copper trees into the Bowl, where I had my first opportunity to begin placing plants. It was a small start, but I now began to feel what the garden would be like, and I was eager to begin with Irwin the dance of actively placing each and every plant.

Following quickly, pink-flowered crape myrtles were set out in the middle and upper planting rings surrounding the Bowl. Again, boxed specimens were lifted into place and set at precise elevations by use of transit and laser. The remaining soil mix was then deposited carefully around the root balls of the trees. At the same time, another planting ring, which encircled the lower part of the Bowl Garden, was filled with soil. In each of these rings a different plant was used en masse. An intricate part of Irwin's plan was (and still is) for the colors in the Bowl to rise up over the spring and summer. First the azaleas bloom in March, the kalanchoe in April and May, and the tulbaghia in June and July, while the crape myrtles bloom all summer. Gray-leaved *Kalanchoe pumila* clothe the lower ring, variegated society garlic (*Tulbaghia violacea*) the middle ring, and three types of New Zealand flax (*Phormium*)—in bronze, green, and brown tones—fill the larger upper ring. Irwin spent days in laying out precise geometries so that each of the three rings would radiate in curving lines outwardly from the rings of the azalea maze. I myself spent hours laying out wooden forms, one-by-twelve-inch pine boards cut with appropriate arcs and notched for plant location. Workmen could then swiftly and accurately place the thousands of one-gallon plants required. Surveyors laid out top and bottom marks on the rings so the forms could be moved, line by line, ensuring precise placement.

As the rings took shape, work on the hardscape areas of the Stream Garden was in full swing. We established grade as soon as the cranes working on the nearby buildings completed their work. A rough channel was cut, snaking down the slope for the future stream. Now we could visualize its size and scope. Irwin was everywhere during the construction phase, watching and directing every possible detail of design. He stood out in his chic straw hat, worn to protect him from the sun, atop which he also wore the mandatory hard hat. At the time I think Bob was sixty-eight or sixty-nine years old, yet he outpaced workers half his age. I am a fairly strong worker myself, and he routinely ran me into the ground. Earlier in the year he had visited a wholesale nursery in Santa Barbara. Irwin began the visit in the morning and spent the entire day, nonstop, walking the vast grounds, inspecting each plant. He had to be asked to leave at the five o'clock closing. More than once I had to say, "Bob, I'm worn out, let's go home." Partially responsible for his impressive energy level may be the perennial glass of Coke and ice always within reach. (Note: The correct type of ice is paramount.)

It was now time for Irwin to install the rock sculpture that was be the focal point in the Stream Garden. Most designers would opt for a realistic stream, but Irwin used this opportunity to create a sculpture, in the form of a stream, upon which to base this part of the garden. There was considerable consternation among the contractors. As Irwin had never actually worked with rock and water before, many quietly predicted failure. Huge blocks of green chert, from the Gold Country of California, were scattered all over the upper slopes. Irwin walked up and down this handpicked collection of rocks, sizing up and choosing each rock for its fit, as if he were putting together a huge jigsaw puzzle. At the top of the stream the boulders would dominate, obscuring the water below. Smaller pieces of rock cemented together were placed below to create sound channels. Farther down the stream sculpture the boulders were carefully and more openly placed for the water to rush out and around. Near the bottom of the stream the boulders were to disappear completely, letting the water be the primary focus. It was great theater watching this unfold.

With the stream in place a dual allée of London plane trees, specifically grown for the project, were craned into position along the earth berms bordering the stream. (We had built up berms underneath the trees with the desired soil mix.) This was a turning point, for now the cranes could be withdrawn from the garden. These large specimen trees really turned the bare area into a living space by supplying the necessary scale and structure to act in counterpoint to the surrounding architecture.

We now prepared for the big push: we could finally plant the garden. Some 70 percent of the plants were to come from my growing grounds, while the rest would be ordered in. At first I began trucking the plants from Encinitas myself. Renting my favorite fifteen-foot truck and installing the shelves became a weekly ritual. It was soon apparent that I would not have enough time to truck in all the plants. December was not far away; it would be a miracle if we were ready for the opening. And it seemed the whole world was waiting for this event. Legions of press had already prepared stories for the evening news; every TV channel I turned to was talking about the Getty. Hundreds of prominent people were expected, and we didn't want to disappoint them. At the same time Irwin had taken to heart the admonition that you can't create a great garden by following the current fashion in landscape practice, which is to bring in everything full grown and simply roll it out. He saw this as a critical question of values, and we made a major decision when we opted to begin by growing the trees and plants in the garden.

There were irrigation problems in the Bowl Garden, so I began setting plants in the stream first. I drew the plan, knowing what the Stream was going to look like, but Irwin couldn't visualize the concept through the drawings. So first I set each potted plant into its position before actual planting commenced: an odd approach, but Irwin needed to be able to see and suggest modifications. To hasten the delivery of plants from Encinitas we hired a full-sized semitruck and trailer to bring the plants up. The company was purportedly reliable and set up to move containerized plants. While I was at the Getty the trucks arrived in Encinitas. When wholesalers make deliveries to my nursery, their trucks always have numerous and secure shelves, and I anticipated the same from this company. But these trucks arrived with practically no shelving. My workers did their best to brace the weak shelves that were supplied. Late in the afternoon the truck and trailer arrived at the site and the first trailer was backed into position. I had twenty workers there to help unload and move the plants. The first truck was opened and unloading commenced; we had a lot of material here, rare and unusual material. Then the second trailer was moved in and I walked over to open the doors. My heart fell to the ground when the doors opened: all the shelving had collapsed onto itself. More than a year of work, collecting and growing, lay mangled before me. In a daze I began to pull the broken lumber and flattened plants from the truck, but I was overwhelmed by the disaster.

I stepped back to let our crew finish the job, watching in disbelief as prized plants emerged from the pile.

The following morning I surveyed the damage, swallowed hard, and continued to place plants in the stream. I had no choice but to use some of these battered plants, because there were no others available. I made many frantic calls trying to locate replacements. Time was running short, the weather became increasingly berserk with strong winds and flooding rains, and many of my plants were in less than pristine condition. On one stormy day, in full rain gear, nearly the only one still working, I found myself pulling my nursery wagon loaded with plants and gear, leaning forty-five degrees into gale-force winds and rain. The fury of the storm nearly knocked me down. I finally gave in, abandoned my gear, and headed for my hotel room.

With plants still in their pots and set in a stream, Irwin and I made a final assessment. We moved some things around, but in general he felt we were ready to plant. Even as the plants were finding their homes, the excitement of opening day was increasing. There were many pre-opening events. Various groups were invited to tour parts of the museum and stroll the marble hallways. For three days in a row, press from around the world descended on the new buildings. Here a reporter from Venezuela directed his viewers around the central plaza, while a Japanese camera crew shot the tram arriving. Though the Stream Garden was unfolding, only a handful of plants had been set out in the Bowl; our work was far from complete. With the grand opening only days away, many important features were still unfinished. Irwin had designed special lights for the garden but was forced to use temporary replacements so that visitors would be able to walk through the garden on opening night. There were continuing problems with the irrigation system, and the plants had to be hand-watered for several months. It wasn't possible to finish the Bowl Garden, and the plants were lined up on the paths in nursery-like fashion. It couldn't be helped, and we continued to plant after opening day. There was so much press, so much anticipation, that the Getty was inundated with people, far more than expected. Literally tens of thousands of people lined up to see and experience the marble-clad Museum and the surrounding buildings. Irwin and I found ourselves working on the Bowl Garden right in the middle of all the excitement. It would take much of January to complete the initial installation.

There was a curious juxtaposition of feelings present in those early days. On more than one occasion, while Irwin and I were putting together the Bowl Garden, the new visitors would applaud us with hearty handclaps. Considering the constraints of time, weather, and various uncontrollable disasters, we both felt that the garden was working well. There were some mistakes, especially in the Bowl, where the plant composition was not as clear as we would have liked, but the underlying design ideas were, and are, exciting and novel. Irwin had something here, something not seen in previous public gardens, something that truly is art.

In the following years it has become my job to direct the care and growth of the new garden. I come to the site every other week, bringing new plants and helping to train the crew. The Getty is closed on Mondays, so I find that day of the week a rare treat, as I can walk through the Central Garden when it is empty of visitors. Around three o'clock, when the crew departs, I have the whole place to myself. I sit on one of the teak benches and let my mind wander over the extraordinary sights before me.

A WALK THROUGH THE GETTY GARDEN

Our journey begins from an overlook that offers a tantalizing vista of the whole garden space. The garden sits in an area dominated by the surrounding architecture, which rests on top of a U-shaped crest. Robert Irwin's design for the garden relates both visually and physically to the grandeur of the site. He chose hardscape materials that reflect the extraordinary craftsmanship and detail found in the Getty Center's buildings. Teak and bronze play against finely cut stone, while lush plantings offset rusty-colored Cor-Ten steel.

Irwin offers the visitor a series of sensory engagements that reflect his approach to the elements of perception. First there are the London plane trees, *Platanus* × *acerifolia* 'Yarwood', which line each side of the stream. Chosen for their unique structural character, these trees form a giant hedge, forty feet tall and wide, that is trimmed flat on the sides and top. Careful pruning keeps their skeletal structure open, allowing light to reach the diverse planting below. The London plane trees are set twenty-two feet apart in each direction. This creates a formality for the stream, defining it as a line or channel rather than a meandering brook. Irwin's stream is sculptural, formed of rock, a green chert from the Gold Country of California. At the top of the stream the rocks are more massive and set tightly together. You can hear the water splashing below, but you cannot see it. Farther down, the water bubbles up and spills over a rock edge, the way many springs start in nature. Midway in the stream, boulders are more widely spaced, with the water coursing between them. Farther on, the rocks diminish in size and number as the water itself becomes the key visual element. Toward the bottom of the stream the rocks disappear completely, and the water races down a V-shaped culvert lined with flat stones set on edge. Irwin has taken the formal channel and layered it into a series of events, each offering some new discovery.

Outside of Irwin's grand hedge are twenty-foot swaths of deergrass, *Muhlenbergia rigens*, a California native with soft arching blades and narrow, erect flowering spikes. This homogenous planting adds a layer to the slim line of the stream, expanding the width of the garden area under the London plane trees. Irwin looked at many different grasses and eventually singled out deergrass because it holds its stately character nearly year-round.

A switchback descends through the deergrass and the tree-lined stream. The path is laid in a herringbone design, with elegant blue stone from the mountains of

Pennsylvania. At the stream crossing, teak planks, cut half the width of the stone, repeat the herringbone pattern. A bronze grate spans the areas where the two materials meet, knitting them together, so to speak. Irwin held the width to four feet, allowing for the flow of visitors. Descending at a defined gradient, the path cuts into the sloping ground, where it is lined with a slim retaining wall of Cor-Ten steel. Cor-Ten develops a violet-brown patina, creating the effect that the earth has simply been cut away to form the path, adding strength to the garden and reflecting the geometric character of the surrounding buildings. Plants will be encouraged to spill over the edges, softening them as only nature can.

Plantings in the Stream Garden, displayed in twelve-foot-wide berms on each side of the stream, are a study of leaves; in this part of the garden, flowers are only bonuses. Irwin allows the color and texture of leaves to paint the canvas. His plan divides the Stream Garden into four subtle areas, creating an almost subliminal understructure. Unlike most gardeners—who find a plant and then try to fit it into their garden—Irwin first establishes conditions and then searches for plants that will satisfy them. Beginning in Area 1, at the top of the stream, the plants are displayed in carpet-like fashion, closer and tighter to the ground. Echeverias laid out in geometric precision greet the visitor at the outset. Leaf colors in all the plants are in homogenous shades of gray, gray green, and yellow green. Gray is a muted color that can be enlivened or dampened by the presence of other colors. Irwin calls these other colors the "kicker" colors, as they activate the palette, putting the grays in motion. A kicker color needs to be both compatible with and able to intensify the main color. In Area 1, the chartreuse coloring of *Sedum confusum*, *Lysimachia nummularia* 'Aurea', *Plectranthus forsteri* 'Gigantea Aurea', and *Agapanthus* 'Stripes' are the kickers and provide the excitement for the various shades of gray. As a bonus, Irwin sought the punch of orange flowers for this area. Brilliant California poppies do the job part of the year. But for effect year-round, the orange and green leaves of *Carex testacea* and *Libertia peregrinans* provide the kicker color. Giving scale to the carpeting plants are the taller gray leaves of *Lavandula* 'Goodwin Creek'. Its soft, airy, purple flower spikes dance in the breeze. Just off the walkway, orange thorns of *Solanum pyracanthum* surprise visitors. An unusual member of the potato family, this solanum shares its cousin's flower shape and soft lavender coloring. When I found this plant in a nursery, I knew that Irwin would like it because of its unique look. Visitors comment on this plant daily, always quizzing the crew as to its name and culture. Past the solanum is the first of five teak bridges that cross the stream, where large blocks of green chert are massed on either side.

As we continue down the monochromatic blue-stone path and cross the second bridge we are surrounded by Area 2. Here the plants are taller, leaving a "window" space under the tree branches that frames the view. Gray greens and gray blues dominate the leaf coloring. *Euphorbia characias* subsp. *wulfenii* and the newer cultivar *E.* 'Jade Dragon' provide these colors. Irwin chose blue green as the desired kicker color, although it can be a very difficult color to find in plants. During a plant trip to Oregon I found the rare variegated form of the Corsican hellebore, *Helleborus argutifolius* 'Janet Starnes'. Its lime-green flowers complement the blue green, and the white speckled blue-green leaves may be a near perfect choice for the kicker. A specimen of *Astelia* 'Silver Spear', with its brilliant silver-gray leaf, adds lightness to the palette. Irwin's bonus flower color here is the clear brilliant yellow found in the Mexican tulip poppy, *Hunnemannia fumariifolia*. Beyond the bridge, the first of two sculptured teak benches is wrapped by curved and mitered Cor-Ten steel.

A small island bed across from the teak seat contains three specimen plants of *Dudleya pulverulenta*. A native Californian, chalk lettuce is difficult to grow, requiring careful watering. We planted the large rosettes on a slope and tilted them at an angle to prevent water from collecting in the crown. Our method of planting helps this drought-tolerant plant withstand the regular watering the garden receives. This technique is not foolproof but opens the door for using this deserving beauty in a garden setting.

Past the enticing seating and the island bed is a subtle grouping that features the smaller variety of *Astelia* 'Red Gem', surrounded by black mondo grass (*Ophiopogon planiscapus* 'Nigrescens'). Glowing grassy tufts of *Deschampsia cespitosa* 'Northern Lights' accent the composition. Below, hugging the stream, is silvery *Convolvulus cneorum*, the 'Bush Morning Glory', which carries sparkling white flowers. Often difficult plants to grow, these are also planted on a slope. In the light shade of the London plane trees the silver foliage and glowing white flowers give the eye a very special treat. Contrasting well with the white Bush Morning Glory are the large purple daisy flowers of *Arctotis* 'Torch Purple'. Blooming nonstop for months, this South African perennial is a premier ground cover.

These purple daisies can be admired from the third bridge. Here the stream opens up as the imposing stacks of granite fade away. Water splashes openly around the remaining rocks. Leaving the stream for a while, the path cuts through the deergrass and into the surrounding slope. You turn a corner and discover that this new stretch offers the longest line of sight as it slices diagonally through the third area of plantings.

Your senses are enveloped in lush verdant greens, some with purple-black accents. White and rich red are the flower colors in this section, while the kicker color is kelly green. Tall stems of *Canna* 'Black Knight' feature dark green leaves and red flowers of intense full hue. Height is important here in Area 3, and the visitor is enveloped by luxuriant foliage, emphasizing the feeling of being surrounded, being completely inside. Plant material is allowed to grow right up to the lower tree limbs. A second curved teak bench lies at the edge of the stream. Here the viewer can appreciate the sweet, subtle fragrance of the heliotrope 'Black Beauty' in contoured comfort. The purple-black leaves and rich purple flowers of the 'Black Beauty' accent the clear white 'Iceberg' roses. The ground is covered in *Thymus* 'Coconut', a fine, low-growing selection that is also one of the easiest thymes to cultivate.

On the far side of the stream, lace-cap hydrangeas contrast with the tropical purple leaves of *Crinum asiaticum cupreifolium*. These very ornamental crinums hold large lavender flowers on tall sturdy spikes. Old-fashioned Lenten roses, *Helleborus argutifolius*, spotlight lime-green flowers that bring constant comment from visitors. Now the stream rushes freely under a fourth bridge, splashing over the last small blocks of green chert. The stream becomes a V-shaped channel open to the water's dancing rush. Past the bridge, the blue-stone path runs out into deergrass and into the turf in one long gentle slope. A final switchback to the path is lined with curved Cor-Ten steel. The gentle curve tempers the inherent strength of the steel. Seeing the craftsmanship involved is rewarding in itself.

Excitement and exuberance lie ahead as the plantings lining the stream reach a crescendo. Irwin's design for Area 4 is fully alive, dancing and bright with color. Here we offer a greater variety in the character and color of leaves, a lively mix of greens that includes bright greens, yellow greens, and gray greens. If there were a kicker color here it would have to be the brightest green, a chartreuse yellow green. We find purple heliotrope spilling over the golden-green foliage of *Campanula* 'Dickson's Gold'. Golden thyme, *Thymus aureus*, flows around bronze-leaved *Phormium* 'Jack Spratt'. Billowing mounds of coral fountain grass, *Russelia equisetiformis*, cascade into the stream. Brilliant orange tiger lilies pop above golden-leaved breath of heaven, *Coleonema pulchrum* 'Golden Sunset'. A garland of nasturtium, with orange blossoms, encircles the large verdant green leaves of *Geranium maderense*, the largest true geranium. The nasturtium softly cradles mint-green hellebores and is backlit with the stunning purple-red leaves of *Phormium* 'Guardsman'. There are no timid combinations in Area 4. Here the berm plantings are alive with color and striking in texture.

Finally the Stream Garden plantings end as they spread out onto sand-colored D.G. (decomposed granite) and into an invitingly large open plaza. In early plans the garden ended at the plaza. Irwin fought hard to expand what would have been a truncated space in order to meet the Trust's own desire for a truly public, friendly place. In the final plan the garden is nearly twice as big as it was originally, with the treasured addition of the circular Bowl Garden that extends out from the plaza.

After touring the Stream Garden, the plaza is a place where the visitor can pause to contemplate the journey taken. But more surprises gather around this meeting area. First to be encountered are the bougainvillea bowers, fifteen-foot-tall umbrella-shaped stands that support multiple plantings of bougainvilleas. Several colors are intermingled in each of the bowers. These are constructed of one-inch rebar forming a cone that flares out into a flattened umbrella. There are three umbrellas on each side of the stream, and they act as pegs that link the Stream and Bowl Gardens together. At the base of each set of bougainvilleas are six planting areas, each filled with a different ground cover. On one side of the stream the combination features *Origanum* 'Jim Best', a golden-leaved cultivar; *Calylophus drummondianus*, with its bright yellow flowers; gold-green *Campanula* 'Dickson's Gold'; *Limonium psilocladium*, a low-growing, mound-forming, rich green statice; flat-growing *Dymondia margaretae*, with its silver leaves; and lastly the brushy *Equisetum scirpoides*, with its deep green stems.

Under the umbrellas, wicker French café chairs are provided for rest and comfort. In the distance, a large bridge arches over the rippling stream. The stream here is shallow and flat as it playfully etches its way across the plaza, to disappear under the bridge. One side of the bridge supports a geometric railing, which is often covered with a dramatic annual vine, *Ipomoea lobata*, or Spanish flag. Brilliant yellow-orange flowers with a crimson cast—a plant I discovered at a small nursery in San Francisco—cover the railing in summer.

The flower-clad bridge demands your attention, stirring you from your chair. On the far side of the plaza are several wide curving steps that lead you down to a wall of cut red carnelian granite. Here is a more intimate view of the water as it rushes by and tumbles over the granite wall. Twenty feet below is Irwin's floating azalea maze. The element of surprise reaches a climax in the Bowl Garden, with Irwin's controversial azalea maze spread out before you. Here is a large circular pool containing a maze constructed of three interlocking sets of circles. The effect is of ripples made by a stone tossed in the water. Planted with azaleas, a different color in each, the waterproofed planters appear to float in the eighteen-inch-deep pool. Visitors toss coins into the water for good luck. It is at this point that the elements of design, water, color, and sound appear to fuse seamlessly, creating a powerful sense of destination, at the same time offering an enticing new set of experiences.

Surrounding the azalea pool is the Bowl Garden, a series of concentric rings, all stepping up from the center and filled with hundreds of perennials and shrubs. From the overlook the sight of so many flowering plants causes the viewer to search for a route into this treasure. On either side of the plaza is a wide path, canopied with pink-flowered crape myrtles. Under the crape myrtles, forming a circle that surrounds the entire Bowl Garden and plaza, is a planting of New Zealand flax. The rim of this outer planting area is raised above the surrounding grass, creating a visual wall that encloses the Bowl. Three colors of phormiums in bronze, brown, and green are intermixed ('Surfer', 'Jack Spratt', and 'Tiny Tim'). This planting unifies the garden by joining the plaza and Bowl. In late afternoon, the sun backlights the phormiums and sends the earth tones into a sparkling song. The lower side of the path, under the crape myrtles, is planted with silver-gray variegated society garlic, *Tulbaghia violacea* 'Silver Lace'. Both the flax and the society garlic are set in spiraling rows that emanate from the center of the maze. There is a third ring of radiating lines, just above the azalea pool, planted with gray *Kalanchoe pumila*. It complements the granite wall with its reddish tone in winter and blushes with pink flowers in spring. Such mass plantings require tough, easy-to-grow plants so that an obvious gap does not develop in the pattern. On the far side of the Bowl, the mass plantings give way to sand-colored gravel. Irwin makes this pause in order to raise the Cor-Ten into a sculptural element. It comes out of the ground for a moment, appearing to crisscross at the entrance to the Bowl Garden.

This walkway, a crisply framed zigzag path, is composed of several bridges that lead down into the Bowl Garden. Irwin's bridges are like a carefully fitted Chinese puzzle, and the zigzag paths repeat the pattern of the Stream Garden. At the center of the first bridge is a space Irwin calls the "Power Spot." Here is the central axis of the garden: amazing flower beds on each side, the azalea pool below, the waterfall directly ahead, and the Stream Garden in the distance, a series of rings radiating out to the surrounding beauty of the architecture. The paintings and sculpture displayed in the Museum nearby elicit wonder, but this spot brings together so many elements of the Getty Center that it, too, creates a sense of revelation.

Entering the Bowl we begin the final act of Irwin's garden play. Unlike the stream, where Irwin focuses on leaves, the Bowl Garden is a study of flowers. Plants are set out on either side in dual, crescent-shaped beds. There is nothing quite as brilliant as a great flower, and here the sculptural elements become the background while the flowers take center stage. First are the big visual events, such as viewing the whole garden from the overlook at the top of the stream. Then come the midlevel events, gained while walking down the blue-stone path. And finally there are the small events, such as seeing a flower close up in the Bowl Garden. You start out with a general kind of looking and—when you make it down into the Bowl—reach a level at which a special flower can be viewed intimately. The last and greatest surprise, after being drawn into the Bowl, is the sight of these striking plants. It's like opening a jewelbox.

As with the Stream Garden, Irwin divides the jewel-like Bowl Garden into four areas. These divisions reinforce the geometry of the site on a new level, a subliminal and artistic level that allows the planting of the flowers to court chaos in its exuberance. Irwin features changes in hue, value, and intensity here. The various colors are defined in terms of hue. Value is the darkness or lightness of the color; intensity is its brightness. When a visitor enters the Bowl, the first area, Area 9, is bright and alive: perennials dance with exuberance, and shrubs riot in colorful abandon. Here is a full range of hues, at maximum intensity and spanning the entire range of values. There is no kicker color in this area, for all the colors are equally vibrant. A brilliant red rose, *Rosa* 'Trumpeter', takes the immediate stage. This two-and-a-half-foot bush is covered with blooms for months on end and rarely suffers from disease; it is a near-perfect rose. Many traditional gardening rules are broken here. Between the roses, spiky orange *Libertia peregrinans* boldly anchors blue Stokes asters, *Stokesia laevis*. Giving height to the bed is a specimen copper tree, *Euphorbia cotinifolia*. Reaching into its bronzy leaves, pink butterflies of *Gaura* 'Siskiyou Pink' dance happily. Upright blue Canterbury bells, *Campanula latifolia*, complement golden feverfew. *Canna* 'Technicolor'—a stunning, variegated two-foot dwarf perennial—resides at the base of a teak trellis that is cloaked in Spanish flag. In summer, giant dahlias (Irwin's tribute to Monet's garden) rise above a golden sea of the sweet potato, *Ipomoea* 'Margarita'. The chartreuse-lined leaves of *Geranium* 'Ann Folkard' mingle with the deep green foliage of 'Trumpeter' roses. For Irwin, the garden is most successful when the flowers and plants weave together in this way, forming a rich, multicolored tapestry.

Further into the garden the plants are grouped in larger numbers, in a more field-like display, with the dominant colors being blue and blue violet. In this section, Area 8, the use of similar and more homogenous colors lightens the hue. Values are kept to the middle range, with no big swings from dark to light. Intensity, or brightness, is also kept in a midrange level. Leaves play in verdant tones similar to the scheme of Area 3 in the Stream Garden. Deep purple spikes of *Salvia* 'May Night' complement the soft violet *Salvia* 'Purple Rain'. Rich red yarrow, *Achillea* 'Red Beauty', surrounds purple *Alstroemeria* 'Rachel'. Pale blue Cupid's dart, *Catananche caerulea*, shoots up between the pink globes of sea thrift, *Armeria maritima*. The deep red leaves of *Lobelia* 'Queen Victoria' intertwine with purple-flowered *Verbena bonariensis*. This verbena with its meandering habit is a favorite of Irwin's. His vision for a small-scale garden tree is realized by *Rosa* 'Meidiland Red' and *Rosa* 'Sea Foam', each grown on five-foot stems. Each rose is trained to arch over an umbrella-like support. Rich reds and dazzling white are the kicker colors used on the west side of the Bowl. On the east side, *Cosmos* 'Sunny Orange-Red' provides the kicker color. Contrary to its name, this cosmos is really a clear orange in color. The interaction of color and texture is more quiet and restful here, drawing one in deeper, calming the senses.

Beyond this quiet there is a pause in activity, a buffer area of gray-toned plantings. Area 7, the smallest area, is a study in subtle background coloring. There is a different strategy here, with really no kicker color and only a few jewel-like surprises. Silver-gray leaves of *Lavandula* 'Goodwin Creek' serve to anchor the double white Shasta daisies, *Leucanthemum* 'Esther Read'. Felty-gray *Lychnis coronaria*, Maltese cross, with its deep maroon flowers, rises with a soft yellow strawflower, *Bracteantha bracteata* 'Soft Yellow'. The airy, textured spikes of *Linaria purpurea* 'Natalie' combine with blue-flowered *Salvia chamaedryoides*. Silver-gray *Tanacetum ptarmiciflorum*, a rare selection from the Canary Islands, carries clouds of white flowers when in bloom. Two five-foot standards, a purple-blossomed princess flower, *Tibouchina urvilleana*, and a white *Rosa* 'Sea Foam', add scale and height. Area 7—raised to waist height to allow for the planting of special specimens—is small but gem-like, a gem that is uncovered only by the earlier journey through all the previous areas of the garden. This is pivotal to Irwin's plan, drawing the visitor subtly from the larger vision to the smaller, more personal experiences of perception.

Across the path is the final planting section, Area 6. Here Irwin's design reflects the implied strength found in the backdrop wall of deep red carnelian granite. Flowers are not preeminent here; the colors and textures of foliage take the stage. Leaves with dark colors are highlighted, as with the purple-black *Hebe* 'Amy' and the lacy black foliage of *Anthriscus* 'Ravenswing'. The reddish purple *Berberis* 'Purple Cloak' is accented by splashes of the rich green foliage of the red-flowered daylily, *Hemerocallis* 'Red Tet'. The ground is covered with purple-leaved *Ajuga* 'Catlin's Giant'.

A bronze-leaved acalypha combines with heavenly bamboo, *Nandina* 'Moyer's Red'. Spring finds the purple tulip, *Tulipa* 'Negrita', mixing with an occasional white 'Shirley' tulip. On the west side, *Rosa* 'Meidiland Red' rises on a five-foot stem. This area is strong on several levels, not only in terms of dark colors but also in plant height. Several dark-leaved cannas emphasize the red granite. *Canna* 'Red Stripe', with its deep green foliage striped with red, and *Canna* 'Intrigue', with its dark green leaf, anchor the ends of the beds. The bold, richly variegated leaves of *Canna* 'Phaison' blend with the purple-green leaves of *Crinum asiaticum cupreifolium*. Rich red *Lobelia* 'Queen Victoria' adds the appropriate kicker color for the dark-foliaged plants. Orange-flowered *Cosmos* 'Sunny Orange-Red' acts as a counterpoint to the brown-violet shading of *Strobilanthes isophyllus*. This strong, contemplative area relies on texture and leaf color to convey its message.

The adventure repeats through the four areas as the U-shaped path reaches a lower level. Here the plants and flowers are viewed more at eye level, offering a very personal measure of sensory engagement. Irwin has taken the visitor from grand views down to the most intimate visual encounter. Leaf and flower, texture and hue, beckon for your attention. A tapestry, woven by an artist and a gardener, lies unfurled from the travertine walls. Each underlying thread is connected to a perceptual process that Irwin has cultivated for a lifetime. This unique viewpoint then joins with the mercurial qualities that gardens—by their very nature—possess. The process is at once a passion and a challenge that together, we hope, have created art.

A GUIDE TO
THE PLANTS IN
THE GETTY'S
CENTRAL GARDEN

NOTES TO THE READER

WATERING

The answer to the question of how often to water will vary by circumstance. Sites and soils vary; sun and shade change with the seasons. Check soil for moisture by digging down a few inches. A soil probe is a great investment as the surface condition rarely tells you what's happening at root level.

Roots seek out moisture and resist growing into dry areas. They will also drown if kept too wet. So spend some time to learn about the soil in your garden.

New plantings need more frequent irrigation to become established. Keep the root mass moist to start; pretend it's still in a pot by building a small dam around the root ball and directing water to it. As the roots grow out, becoming established, you can reduce the frequency of watering.

Here is the general pattern for watering that is used in the catalogue that follows:

Regular water: Every three days.

Average water: Every three to four days.

Moderate water: Every four to five days, or longer when fully established.

FLOWERING TIMES

Bloom periods given here are for coastal Southern California.

TEMPERATURES

All temperatures given are Fahrenheit.

FERTILIZING

At my retail nursery, people often ask if their new plants need fertilizer and if so, what kind to use. I answer with a question. How often do you like to eat? Once a month or every day? And of course we all like to eat frequently, even snacking throughout the day. Plants are really no different. Applying fertilizer at low doses frequently is better than applying a lot of fertilizer occasionally. Give your plants regular, low doses of fertilizer. Feed them and they will be happy.

For liquid fertilizers use one-quarter strength every one to two weeks, or as often as you can. For pelletized, slow-release fertilizer, the dosage is already fixed, so apply the quantity suggested.

CHANGES IN THE GARDEN

Gardening is a lesson in the mercurial qualities of nature. Change is everywhere. This book is based upon my personal experience and is meant to be a guide, not a bible. Bob Irwin and I continuously seek out new plants that offer better solutions to the art concepts he addresses. So, when you visit the Getty, don't be surprised if you can't find every plant described here or if you see a plant not described in the following pages.

LOCATION OF PLANTS

At the end of each plant description is a number or numbers that refer to the section of the garden where that particular plant can be found. A map of the ten sections appears on page 138.

Abelia × *grandiflora*. GLOSSY ABELIA.

3–5 ft. (Garden origin)

Abelias are evergreen shrubs with arching branches. These two selections have white flowers, which add a sparkling effect to the leaves during peak flowering summer through fall. When pruning, occasionally trim the entire stem down to the ground, allowing fresh colorful stems to emerge. As with other abelias, these selections tolerate most soils and moderate watering and thrive in either full sun or light shade. Evergreen or partially deciduous in colder areas and probably hardy to about 20°.

A 'AUREA'. GOLDEN ABELIA. Glossy green leaves that are heavily splashed with yellow; new growth is accented by a golden hue, with spring adding a pink color to the leaves; white flowers. [4]

B 'CONFETTI'. Dark green leaves edged with creamy white; slower and tighter growth than 'Aurea'; white flowers with a pink tinge. [1, 8]

C *Abutilon* × *hybridum* 'Savitzii' ('Souvenir de Bonn'). FLOWERING MAPLE.

3–4 ft. (Garden origin)

A wonderful selection having brightly variegated leaves predominantly colored creamy white with rich green blotches. The growth habit is upright and fairly dense; plants grow somewhat slowly. Normally abutilons do best in partial shade and always benefit from some tip pruning, which encourages compactness. At the Getty this plant performs well in full sun, where it becomes full and more compact. This selection is shy to bloom but can produce soft orange, bell-shaped flowers in winter. Bud drop can occur in hot, drier areas, especially if given too much sun. Abutilons tolerate most soils and require regular watering to perform well. Hardy to about 20–25°. [2, 9]

D *Acalypha wilkesiana* 'Haleakala'.
COPPERLEAF.

6–8 ft. (Pacific islands)

There are many exotic forms and hybrids of Acalypha with showy leaves. This selection has dark bronze foliage with striking, large leaves having curled edges. In general, acalyphas die back in frost-prone areas; they quickly resprout when the weather warms. This cultivar is somewhat hardier than other acalyphas and is only partially deciduous in coastal areas from January through April. Give COPPERLEAF full sun and heat, a good garden soil, and regular water. Hardy to about 25°. [6]

E *Acer palmatum* 'Sango-Kaku'.
CORAL-BARK MAPLE.

10–15 ft. (Japan, Korea)

We often think of maples as being out of place in our warm, sunny climate. Consider using this selection for striking winter effect as it displays exciting coral-colored bark during winter and spring. Early spring will bring a wonderful addition when the new leaf growth emerges a stunning yellow green. Although the maple is graceful during spring and early summer, our summer heat is tough on the leaves and tends to burn them late in the year. To limit leaf-tip burn, give the maple ample water throughout the growing season. Plant in an area where it will be protected from afternoon sun, as this will also help prevent leaf burn. CORAL-BARK MAPLE can give the garden a good nine months or more of beauty—not bad for a plant that should not grow here. Hardy to about –5°. [9]

F VAR. *DISSECTUM* 'EVER RED'. This red-leaved variety with finely dissected leaves is planted in the Stream Garden and is shaded by the LONDON PLANE TREES. The leaves burn only a little during late summer. [3]

Achillea millefolium. COMMON YARROW.

Flowers to 2 ft. (Temperate regions of the Northern Hemisphere)

Yarrows are tough, drought-tolerant perennials with feathery, fine-cut leaves. They form large spreading clumps. Control the size by dividing yearly. Flat-topped clusters of flowers rise on narrow stalks in spring, with peak flowering during summer and sporadically into fall. Plant in full sun with well-drained soil and provide moderate water. Hardy to at least 0°.

Ⓐ 'LAVENDER BEAUTY'. Clean lavender flowers. [9]
Ⓑ 'PAPRIKA'. An excellent reddish bronze with green leaves. [9]
Ⓒ 'RED BEAUTY'. Rich red flowers and dark green leaves. [8]

Acorus gramineus. JAPANESE SWEET FLAG.

8–10 in. × clumping (Eastern Asia)

Clumping, grasslike plant with dense fans of narrow leaves. JAPANESE SWEET FLAG is a good accent for light shade and moist areas. Plants will tolerate most soils but need regular watering to look good. If the leaf tips scorch from too much sun or too little water, JAPANESE SWEET FLAG can be cut back hard to the ground, and fresh new growth will return. Succeeds in those persistently wet areas of the garden. Hardy to at least 0°.

Ⓓ 'OGON'. GOLDEN VARIEGATED SWEET FLAG. Variegated medium yellow and green; a little brighter color is achieved with morning sun. [4, 9]
Ⓔ 'VARIEGATUS'. WHITE-STRIPED JAPANESE SWEET FLAG. Variegated off-white and green. [4, 9]

Ⓕ *Adenanthos drummondii*. WOOLLYBUSH.

3 × 5 ft. (Western Australia)

A small evergreen shrub with striking foliage having light gray-green leaves that are slightly hairy. The soft, needlelike leaves tend to obscure the smallish red flowers. Plants have slightly arching stems and tend to form mounds. Requires good drainage and moderate watering and accepts partial shade. In the wild this species lives in sandy soil, but I have used this plant in heavier soils, where it performed well. Hardy to at least 25°. [2, 3]

Agapanthus. LILY OF THE NILE.
(South Africa)
Tough rhizomatous perennials with strap-shaped leaves and
large open umbels of flowers from late spring through summer. Plant in full sun to light shade. They tolerate most soils
and require only moderate watering. The variegated leaf
forms do best in light shade. Hardy to about 5°.

G 'ELAINE'. Flower stalks to 3–4 ft. An excellent deep
blue-purple selection. There really isn't any reason to grow
the pale, washed-out blue varieties when colors like this
exist. Fabulous with Verbena bonariensis. [8]

H 'STREAKS'. Flower stalks to 2½–3 ft. Brilliant white-
variegated leaves with blue flowers; variegation holds well
even in the sun. [4]

I 'STRIPES'. Flower stalks to 2½–3 ft. A pure white-
flowering selection that is graced with cream-white
variegated leaves. The new growth has the brightest
coloring. [1, 2]

J 'TINKER BELL'. Flower stalks to 8–12 in. This striking
dwarf Agapanthus has variegated foliage colored medium
green and edged with white; the flowers are blue. [4, 9]

K *Agrostemma githago* 'Milas'. CORN COCKLE.
2–3 ft. (Mediterranean region)
Striking spring and summer annual that bears 1–2 in.
purple-pink flowers on tall, wiry stems. This is great when
planted between dahlias and other larger-leaved plants
as it weaves with them. Can self-sow in the garden. Seeds
are noxious; not good to eat. Plant in full sun in good soil
and give moderate water. [8, 9]

A *Ajuga reptans* 'Catlin's Giant'.
CARPET BUGLEWEED.
To 1 ft. (Garden origin)

Low-growing perennial ground cover that spreads by long stolons. 'Catlin's Giant' is an unusually large form of Ajuga with dark green leaves heavily splashed with brownish purple. Erect, blue-purple flower stalks appear in spring and sporadically throughout the year. It is one of the easiest Ajuga to grow. CARPET BUGLEWEED will grow in full sun on the coast to light shade elsewhere and requires good drainage with average water. Uniform moisture is important, but wet feet will cause rot. Ajugas are susceptible to root and crown rots in the heat of summer. Plant in very well-drained soil for best success. Hardy to at least 15°. [6]

B *Alonsoa meridionalis.* MASK FLOWER.
1½ ft. (Northwestern South America)

Tender perennials often used as annuals; they produce showy flowers nearly the whole year in our mild climate. The spurred flowers can be orange, red, or pink, but our favorite is orange, which we use in the bright areas of the garden. Cut back old flowers to encourage a bushier plant. Full sun to light shade in good soil with regular water. Hardy to about 20°. [9]

C *Alstroemeria* 'Rachel'. PERUVIAN LILY.
To 2 ft. (South America)

Rhizomatous perennial that can spread prolifically in the garden to form large clumps. Older clumps, which show decline, should be divided, and old, smaller crowns should be removed. The rhizomes should be planted 6–8 in. deep. New plantings often use the first year to establish and produce vigorous clumps in the second year. Once established, the rhizomes can become weedy. Violet flowers begin in spring and can last into fall. Alstroemerias are superb cut flowers, lasting two weeks or more in the vase. Plant in full sun on the coast, but give some protection with light shade inland. Alstroemerias are heavy feeders and require fertile, well-drained soil and average water. Hardy to at least 15°. [8, 9]

D *Alyogyne hakeifolia.*
RED-CENTERED HIBISCUS.
5–8 ft. (Western and southern Australia)

This is a somewhat open, wispy shrub with very narrow leaf lobes. The deep green leaves contrast well with the large yellow flowers, which open best on sunny days from spring through fall. This particular form lacks the typical red center. Adaptable to various growing conditions, it does well in warm dry areas and cooler moist areas. Good drainage is important for success. Plant in full sun or light shade and supply moderate watering. Prune lightly for compactness. Hardy to about 25°. [3]

E *Anagallis monellii.* BLUE PIMPERNEL.
6–8 in. × 1½ ft. (Mediterranean region)

Incredible deep blue, saucer-shaped flowers cover this perennial throughout much of the year. Best planted out as young, fresh plants, as they easily become leggy in pots. Plant in full sun in good to average soil and supply moderate watering. Hardy to about 5°. [8]

F *Anchusa capensis* 'Blue Angel.'
CAPE FORGET-ME-NOT.
1–1½ ft. (South Africa)

'Blue Angel' is a biennial with small, intense, bright blue flowers and deep green, somewhat coarse leaves. Flowering early spring through summer and sporadically into fall. My plants fade each year, so I treat them as an annual, replanting when necessary. Plant in full sun in well-drained soil and supply regular water. Tolerates some frost. [8]

A *Anemone* × *hybrida* 'Honorine Jobert.'
JAPANESE ANEMONE.
　3 ft. (Garden origin)
JAPANESE ANEMONES are easy-growing, fibrous-rooted
perennials that bloom in the fall and that multiply quickly,
spreading by underground rhizomes. This selection has
pure white flowers. Anemones can self-sow in the garden,
adding to the suckering clumps. Plant in full sun on the
coast to light shade inland with well-drained soil and average moisture. The roots are subject to rot in wet soil. Hardy
to about 0°. [3]

B *Angelica pachycarpa.* ANGELICA.
　1½ × 2 ft. (Temperate North America and Asia)
Bold-looking plants with arching, heavily toothed leaves
colored a shiny, rich green. ANGELICA, a biennial, seeds
itself freely in the garden—actually a wonderful habit since
it dies after flowering and it's a stunning plant to have. The
blossoms form a large umbel of tiny white flowers. Plant in
full sun to light shade, in good soil, and give regular water.
Probably hardy to at least 0°. [3]

C *Angelica stricta* 'Purpurea.'
PURPLE-LEAVED ANGELICA.
　1–2 ft. (Temperate Northern Hemisphere)
A selection with bronze-purple leaves. This form has been
shy to bloom here. Plant in full sun to light shade, in good
soil, and give regular water. Hardy to about –15°. [6]

Anigozanthos flavidus. KANGAROO PAW.

To 2 ft. (Southwestern Australia)

Evergreen clumping perennials with IRIS-like foliage that produce tall stalks of furry, clawlike flowers. Flower stalks begin to form in early spring, and blossoms continue into summer and with sporadic flowers through early winter. Cut out old fans after they have flowered and divide every 2–3 years for better growth. Withhold fertilizer and keep on the dry side after flowering when plants seek a rest. Plant in full sun on the coast to light shade elsewhere in well-drained soil and supply moderate watering. Hardy to around 20–25°.

Ⓓ 'BUSH DAWN'. Tall, 4½ ft. stalks with bright yellow flowers. [8, 9]

Ⓔ 'BUSH SUNSET'. Deep green, narrow leaves up to 2 ft. long, deep red flowers with stalks to 4 ft. [3, 8, 9]

Ⓕ *Anthriscus sylvestris* 'Ravenswing'.
BLACK-LEAVED COW PARSLEY.

1 × 1½ ft. (Europe, North Africa, western Asia)

Attractive, clump-forming perennial with finely dissected, fernlike foliage that begins green and ages to purple black. Flower stalks rise to 2 ft. and are topped with small white blossoms in late spring. Declared a noxious weed in the Pacific Northwest, where it grows larger and seeds prolifically. In our climate the plants are smaller, rarely flower, and have never reseeded for me. 'Ravenswing' can be short-lived here. Anthriscus tolerates most soils; likes sun on the coast to light shade inland and needs moderate watering. Seeds must be fresh to germinate. Hardy to at least 5°. [3, 6]

Aquilegia. COLUMBINE.

1 ft. (Temperate Northern Hemisphere)

COLUMBINES are true harbingers of spring for Southern California. These perennials can be short-lived in our warm climate but this should not deter one from having them in the garden, as spring would not be complete without them. Flower buds begin to appear in March with peak flowering May and June. Do not be afraid to use them as annuals. Foliage of COLUMBINES is soft and fernlike in appearance and has graceful flowers rising on erect stems. Copious quantities of seed are easy to germinate; remember not to cover the seeds. Many are deciduous in winter. Plant in full sun on the coast but give light shade inland in fairly well-drained, compost-enriched soil with regular water during the growing season. Quite hardy to 0° or less.

Ⓐ *CHRYSANTHA.* YELLOW COLUMBINE (Rocky Mountains). Large, upright, golden-yellow flowers with very long spurs. [9]

Ⓑ *SIBIRICA.* One of the best rich blue-flowered species with shorter spurs. [8]

Ⓒ *Arabis procurrens* 'Variegata.'
VARIEGATED ROCK CRESS.

1–2 in. × clumping (The Balkans)

Showy, small-scale, mat-forming ground cover with tight rosettes of small, 1 in. leaves brightly variegated with white. Smallish white flowers are displayed on 6 in. stems from January through February and sporadically June to July. Susceptible to crown rots in our climate so I bring in a few fresh plants each year. Plant in full sun on the coast to light shade inland in well-drained soil and supply moderate watering. Hardy to at least 0°. [1]

D *Arctotis* 'Torch Purple.' AFRICAN DAISY.
   1 × 3 ft. (South Africa)
Excellent ground cover with large, purple, 3½ in., daisylike flowers and gray foliage. Plants send out long stolons,
which are best trimmed back regularly for fullness. When
pruning cut back into silvery green wood only, not into
woody areas. Arctotis grows well in full sun or light shade
and needs only moderate water when established. Good
drainage is essential to produce a floriferous plant. Flowering begins in late winter and peaks for many months, finally
slowing down late in summer. Hardy to about 32°. [2, 3]

E *Armeria alliacea.* SEA-PINK.
   6–8 in. × 12 in. (Western Europe to southwestern
   Germany and northern Italy)
My favorite species of SEA-PINK forms clumps of broad
grasslike leaves and sports 10–12 in. narrow stalks topped
with round clusters of pink flowers. The flowering season
is very long, almost continuous along the coast. In their
second year bare spots appear in the center as individual
stems elongate, leaving the older part leafless. I will then
cut back one side of the plant to the crown and plant a
young replacement in the spot, allowing the two to grow
together. Armerias find good drainage essential, grow best
in full sun, and need regular watering to prosper. Hardy to
about 15°. [8]

F *Armeria maritima* 'Rubrifolia.'
THRIFT (or SEA THRIFT).
   3–6 in. (Europe, Siberia, arctic North America)
This is a new selection for me. The tighter and overall smaller character, accented with the rich bronze-red leaves really
caught my attention. Flowers are deep magenta-pink. The culture is the same as Armeria alliacea. Hardy to about 0°. [6]

Ⓐ *Asparagus virgatus.* ASPARAGUS FERN.
3–4 ft. (South Africa)
A soft-looking, much-refined species introduced by Gary
Hammer. Slender, smooth stems and deep green, very airy
narrow foliage add considerable grace to the garden. This
species forms tight clumps and is not terribly weedy, as are
many of its relatives, although it does spread underground
by rhizomes. Orange berries begin to form in early fall and
add color during the winter months. Plant in full sun on the
coast to light shade inland in well-drained soil with moderate watering. Will also thrive in shady areas everywhere.
Tough and reliable yet adding a soft look in the garden.
Hardy to at least 28°. [9]

Ⓑ *Astelia chathamica* 'Silver Spear.'
SILVER SPEAR.
3 ft. (New Zealand)
Resembling a silver-leaved Phormium, this perennial has
3 ft.-long leaves covered with silvery hairs. The leaves are
2–3 in. wide and add a striking statement to the garden.
Plant in full sun on the coast to light shade inland in well-
drained, compost-enriched soil and give regular watering.
Watch for mealybug in the crown. Hardy to maybe 15°.
[2, 7]

Ⓒ *Astelia nivicola* 'Red Gem.' RED GEM.
1 ft. (New Zealand)
RED GEM is a perennial with sword-shaped leaves having
distinct ribs and colored gray with maroon stripes. The arching, somewhat relaxed leaves glisten with soft, silvery hairs.
Plant in full sun on the coast but give plants light shade
inland. Well-drained, compost-enriched soil with regular
water is necessary for good growth. Hardy to maybe 15°.
[2, 7]

❶ *Aster lateriflorus* 'Lady in Black.'
LADY-IN-BLACK ASTER.
3–4 ft. (North America)

Black-green foliage with clouds of small white flowers in
late summer and fall. This is a stunning plant. Introduced by
Dutch growers, LADY-IN-BLACK ASTER is a showstopper
when in bloom. Cut back old flowering stalks and divide
the root crowns of clumps every 2–3 years. Grow in full
sun in well-drained soil and supply average water. Hardy
to about 15°. [6]

❷ *Asteriscus sericeus.* CANARY ISLAND DAISY.
2 ft. (Canary Islands)

Beautiful, light silver-green leaves with a yellowish cast form
a compact bush that seems to always be in flower. Large
2 in., rich yellow blossoms nestle near the surface of the
leaves. Old brown leaves persist but can be pulled off while
grooming. Plant in full sun in average soil and give moderate water to produce good plants. Hardy to about 15°.
[4, 9]

❸ *Athanasia acerosa.* COULTER BUSH.
3–4 ft. (South Africa)

A striking shrub with narrow, silvery gray leaves 3–5 in.
long, which curl at the tips. Accepts pruning well to form a
more compact bush. Unusual clusters of yellow, YARROW-
like flowers begin to form in spring, with peak flowering
May and June. As plants age they form interesting gnarled
trunks. Tolerant of most soils. Plant in full sun and give moderate watering. Hardy to about 25°. [1, 2, 7]

ⓐ *Azorina vidalii.*
AZORES PINK CAMPANULA.
1½ ft. (Azores)

This relative of campanulas has glossy green leaves with serrated edges and produces tall stalks of large, pendent, waxy pink or white flowers that appear first in June, peak in July, and blossom sporadically in August and September. Plant in full sun or light shade in well-drained soil and give average water. Self-sows in the garden to form wonderful colonies. Hardy to at least 25°. [8]

Babiana. **BABOON FLOWER.**
6–15 in. (South Africa)

Babiana are winter- and spring-growing geophytes that are dormant in summer. These varieties can take summer watering. Plant the corm 6 in. deep in full sun or light shade in a very well-drained soil. Babianas can self-sow in the garden. Protect from frost.

ⓑ *RUBROCYANEA.* WINECUPS. Striking flowers of blue-purple with red centers. [7]
ⓒ *STRICTA.* 15 in. Colors varying from white to blue to purple and maroon. [8]

ⓓ *Ballota nigra* 'Archer's Variety.'
BLACK HOREHOUND.
6–12 in. (Europe, North Africa)

A highly ornamental perennial having medium green leaves that are brightly splashed with white. Whorls of attractive purplish flowers decorate the colorful leaves. Plant in well-drained soil in light shade or full sun and give moderate water. Hardy to at least 27°. [2]

E *Bauhinia corymbosa.* PHANERA.

Vine (South China)

This very graceful vine climbs with tendrils, has rounded
1 in. leaves that are twin-lobed, and in summer produces
soft violet flowers that resemble butterflies. Watch for spi-
der mites in warm months. Plant in full sun in well-drained
soil and supply moderate watering to produce good plants.
Can be semideciduous in winter. Hardy to about 25° [7]

F *Begonia* 'Paul Hernandez'.
GIANT BEGONIA.

4–5 ft. (Garden origin)

This is an impressive plant with large leaves (to 15 in.
across) and huge, basketball-sized flower clusters. The
crinkled leaves are a deep earthy green, and the flowers
are white with yellow stamens. Thick stems will need staking
to hold the large leaves and flowers. Plant in average soil
and supply regular water. Best in light shade. Hardy
to at least 28° [2, 3]

G *Begonia* 'Richmondensis'.
SHRUBBY BEGONIA.

1½ ft.–2 ft. (Garden origin)

Everyone grows BEGONIAS, and these are some of the
easiest and most rewarding. We shouldn't be afraid to grow
a plant just because it is common (and neither should we
grow only common plants). The leaves of the selection are
a shiny, waxy red and seem always to be in flower. Good
in light shade or full sun. Plant in average soil and supply
regular water. Hardy to at least 28° [4]

Berberis. BARBERRY.

(Temperate Northern Hemisphere)

These species of BARBERRY are winter-deciduous shrubs with spines along the stems and colorful berries during winter. The dense foliage is set with small roundish leaves. Plant in full sun or light shade in most soils and supply moderate watering. BARBERRY will suffer in drought conditions. Cut back yearly for compactness. Hardy to at least 0°.

Ⓐ *THUNBERGII* **'ROSE GLOW'.** JAPANESE BARBERRY. 3–5 ft. Exciting foliage colored purple-red and marbled with light pink and deep red berries. [8, 9]
Ⓑ *VULGARIS* **'PURPLE CLOAK'.** JAUNDICE BERRY. To 6 ft. Upright growth, deep reddish purple leaves, small yellow flower clusters, and deep red berries. [6, 8]

Ⓒ *Boronia heterophylla.* RED BORONIA.

5–6 ft. (Western Australia)

Deep green, fine, needlelike foliage creates a soft, airy-looking, upright shrub. Brushing the fragrant foliage releases a wonderful aroma. Small deep pink-red, pendulous flowers in spring are very fragrant. Very fast-growing but needs good drainage to survive. Not really drought-tolerant as a regular source of water is essential. Wet feet are certain death. Give the roots a cool location and lean toward the acid side in soil. Beautiful plants, very fragrant but often very finicky. Plant in full sun to light shade. Hardy to about 20°. [3, 8]

Ⓓ *Bracteantha bracteata* 'Soft Yellow.' STRAWFLOWERS.

2–3 ft. (Garden origin)

An amazing selection with gray-green leaves and a nearly continuous display of soft yellow STRAWFLOWERS. The unique flowers have a strawlike texture; they are often used in dry bouquets. Plant in full sun in well-drained soil and supply moderate water. STRAWFLOWERS can be quite drought-tolerant once established. Hardy to about 20°. [7]

❺ *Brugmansia suaveolens* 'Charles Grimaldi.'
GOLDEN ANGELS' TRUMPET.

   To 15 ft. (Garden origin)

Large shrub or small tree with very large, soft yellow-orange,
trumpet-shaped, pendent flowers. 'Charles Grimaldi' is
wonderfully evening-scented and very prolific in flowering,
March to November. With careful pruning ANGELS'
TRUMPET can be trained into very attractive small trees
with flat-topped canopies. Plant in full sun or light shade.
Tolerant of most soils with moderate water. Although damaged by frosts, ANGELS' TRUMPET can recover quickly.
Hardy to about 25°. [9]

❻ *Brugmansia* × *candida* 'Double White.'
WHITE ANGELS' TRUMPET.

   10–15 ft. (Garden origin)

Larger deep green leaves with double white flowers.
Flowering seems to peak May to June and September to
November, with sporadic blossoms at other times. Planted
in full sun or light shade, WHITE ANGELS' TRUMPETS
are very drought-tolerant once established. Hardy to
about 25°. [8]

❼ *Calamintha grandiflora* 'Variegata.'
CALAMINT.

   8–15 in. (Southern Europe)

CALAMINTS are rhizomatous perennial herbs related to
the SALVIAS. This selection has vibrant pink, tubular flowers and lovely serrated, light green leaves generously
splashed with white. Plant in full sun in most soils and with
regular watering to produce good plants. Hardy to 15°. [7]

A *Calandrinia.* CALANDRINIA.
(Western South America)
Calandrinia is a genus of often fleshy-leaved herbs. The species listed below has an especially vivid flower color. Best grown in full sun in average soil with moderate water.

GRANDIFLORA. Blue-gray succulent leaves form low, spreading mounds. Tall airy flower stalks carry iridescent purple flowers that are remarkably long-lasting as a cut flower. Hardy to at least 28°. [2]

B *Callicarpa bodinieri* var. *giraldii* 'Profusion.' BEAUTYBERRY.
6–8 ft. (Western and central China)
BEAUTYBERRY is a deciduous shrub that Robert Irwin uses for its late fall and winter display of bright purple berries. The arching branches are clothed in 4 in., pointed-oval leaves. Plants seem to produce more berries as they get more established in the garden. Plant in full sun to light shade in most soils and supply moderate water. Hardy to about 0°. [2]

Calluna vulgaris. SCOTCH HEATHER.
12–18 in. (Europe and North Africa to Asia Minor)
Small shrubs densely clothed in small, scalelike leaves with dense clusters of small, bell-shaped flowers. SCOTCH HEATHER is a challenging plant in our climate; it requires a well-drained soil leaning to the acid side. Grow in sun or part shade and add generous amounts of peat moss to the soil to make the soil acidic. Fertilize lightly with an acid fertilizer and water moderately. Hardy to about 0°.

C 'PETER SPARKES'. Larger double flowers colored a rose-pink. [1]
D 'TIB'. A little taller than 'Peter Sparkes'; winter months produce copious silver-white flower buds along the stem; in spring the buds open to pink-lavender flowers. Leaves are an earthy green with a bronze edge. [1]

E *Calylophus drummondianus.*
SHRUBBY EVENING PRIMROSE.

1 ft. (Central United States and north central Mexico)
Bright yellow flowers cover the EVENING PRIMROSE for
many months, spring through fall. The leaves of this bushy
Texas plant are very narrow and borne on thin stems that
can root along the soil. Plant in full sun in well-drained soil
and supply average water. Hardy to 15–20°. [5]

Campanula. BELLFLOWER.

(Northern Hemisphere)
Perennials for light shade typically with bell-shaped flowers
in varying shades of blue, purple, and white. Cut back old
stems for repeat blooms. Well-drained soil is essential for
campanulas. Plant in full sun on the coast to light shade
elsewhere and supply regular watering to produce good
plants. Generally hardy to about 0°.

F *GARGANICA* 'DICKSON'S GOLD'. GOLD-LEAVED
ADRIATIC BELLFLOWER (southeastern Italy to western
Greece). Stems to 6 in. A stunning, low-growing selection
with lime-green variegated leaves; blue flowers appear in
May and June; best in light shade. [4, 5]

G 'JOSE'. 2 ft. Upright-growing with large deep blue flowers beginning in late March and lasting into May; if cut
back, a second flush can occur in summer. [9]

H *PORTENSCHLAGIANA.* DALMATION BELLFLOWER. Low
mound to 7 in. Blue-purple flowers on long, twining stems,
which begin in May and last into midsummer. [3]

Canna. CANNA LILY.

(Tropics and subtropics)

CANNA LILIES have thick, tuberous rhizomes and large, tropical-looking foliage. Each has only one flowering stalk but several flowering clusters along that stalk. After all clusters have flowered, cut entire stalk down to ground. CANNA LILIES enjoy a good garden soil with a regular supply of moisture. Flowering can extend from spring through late fall, even early winter. Plant in full sun to light shade. Foliage is damaged by light frosts but the rootstocks are hardy to about 10°.

A 'BLACK KNIGHT'. To 4–5 ft. Deep green leaves with rich red flowers; a very long flowering period in coastal areas. [3]

B 'INTRIGUE'. To 6–8 ft. Dark green leaves; small, light orange flowers. This selection runs fast by having long internodes on the rhizome. [6]

C 'PHAISON'. To 6 ft. Orange flowers with strikingly varie-gated leaves. [6, 9]

D 'PRETORIA'. To 4–5 ft. Orange flowers; leaves flushed yellow and striped with green. [4]

E 'RED STRIPE'. Very tall, to 8 ft. Deep green leaves striped with red; medium orange flowers. [6]

F 'STUTTGART'. Very tall, 6–8 ft. or more. Foliage heavily striped with white; light salmon flowers. [2]

G 'TECHNICOLOR'. To 2 ft. Light pink flowers with boldly variegated leaves. [9]

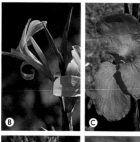

Carex. SEDGE.

(Temperate and arctic zones, higher tropical areas)
A group of grasslike monocotyledons that grow from tight
basal clumps sending out narrow arching leaf blades.
Sedges do best in fairly well-drained soil with regular watering and can be planted in full sun near the coast or light
shade elsewhere. Hardy to around 15°.

H *ELATA* 'AUREA'. BOWLES' GOLDEN SEDGE
(or TUFTED SEDGE). 15–24 in. Bright golden-yellow
leaves form an arching fountain; best grown in light shade
but can take more sun on the coast if given plenty of water;
slow to establish after planting or dividing. [4, 9]

I *HACHIJOENSIS* 'EVERGOLD'. 1 ft. Sparkling white and
green variegation; best in light shade. [2, 8]

J *TESTACEA*. ORANGE-COLORED SEDGE. 1½ × 2 ft.
My favorite accent sedge with showy, medium green leaves
that turn orange as they mature. Best color in full sun but
performs well in light shade, too. [1, 3, 4, 9]

K *Catananche caerulea.* CUPID'S DART.

6 in. with flower stalks 1½–2 ft. (Southwestern Europe)
Once used in love potions, this delightful small-scale perennial carries late spring and summer flowers with a peak May
to July. CUPID'S DART has serrated, gray-green leaves
and forms low clumps. Its papery, lavender-blue flowers are
held high above the foliage and are followed by interesting
papery dry seed pods. Plant in full sun in well-drained soil
and supply moderate watering for a fine perennial at the
front or middle border. Hardy to about 0°. [8, 9]

L 'BICOLOR'. White with blue-purple centers. [7]

M *Centaurea cyanus* 'Black Gem'.
BACHELOR'S BUTTONS.

1–2½ ft. (North temperate regions)
BACHELOR'S BUTTONS is an annual commonly seen in
home gardens. It is easily grown from seed or pony packs
and provides the garden with narrow, gray-green foliage
topped with a myriad of buttonlike flowers. This selection
has dark brown, nearly black blossoms. Plant in full sun in
average soil and give moderate water. In our mild winter
location they can flower summer, fall, and into winter.
Annual. [8]

A *Cercis canadensis* 'Silver Cloud.'
VARIEGATED EASTERN REDBUD.
(North America)
REDBUDS are small to medium-sized trees, often with multiple trunks. This wonderful selection has rounded leaves heavily blotched with white. Deciduous in winter, with rose-pink flowers on bare stems in spring. Probably best with afternoon shade. Needs a good compost-enriched, well-drained soil with regular watering. Hardy to 0° or less. [7]

B *Cerinthe major.* HONEYWORT.
(Mediterranean basin)
Showy annuals with blue-green leaves that support pendent clusters of purple flowers. New plants can be sown any time of the year and will flower fairly quickly. Cerinthe will reseed prolifically in the garden. Plants that have seeded-in give a tremendous display in the cool months of January to March. Plant in full sun or light shade; tolerant of most soils with average water. Very hardy probably to about 20° or less. [1, 2]

C *Cestrum* 'Newellii.' RED CESTRUM.
4–6 ft. (Garden origin)
Blooming almost continuously with a peak in late winter and spring, this superior selection of Cestrum has dark evergreen foliage and very deep red flowers that are followed by rich red berries. This selection branches more freely and is therefore more compact than other species. Pruning helps to create a very full, compact bush. Sun or light shade and regular watering produce a fine plant that is tolerant of most soils. Hardy to about 20°. [3]

Ⓓ *Choisya ternata* 'Sundance'.
MEXICAN MOCK ORANGE.
3–4 ft. (Mexico)

The new growth is a bright golden-yellow on this evergreen,
upright-growing shrub. Plant in light shade where the gold-
en color holds up best. Clusters of fragrant white flowers
appear in midspring. Choisya needs a well-drained soil and
only moderate watering once established. Wonderful for
brightening a shady spot, where it can highlight darker
foliaged plants such as Phormium 'Amazing Red'. Hardy
to about 20–25°. [2, 4]

Ⓔ *Chondropetalum tectorum.*
CAPE RUSH (or ROOF REED).
4–6 ft. (South Africa)

Very ornamental, rushlike plant, technically a restioid, with
long, arching, rounded stems. Small triangular golden
"wings," ¼ in. to ⅜ in. long, adorn the stems along
their length. Deep brown seed heads begin to form in late
summer and are very decorative. Drought-tolerant once
established; plant CAPE RUSH in full sun to light shade
in well-drained soil and supply moderate watering. Hardy
to maybe 20°. [1, 3]

Ⓕ *Clematis tangutica.* GOLDEN CLEMATIS
(or RUSSIAN VIRGIN'S BOWER).
Vine to 10 ft. (Western China)

GOLDEN CLEMATIS is a winter-deciduous vine with
two very ornamental features. An abundance of pendent,
golden-yellow, bell-shaped blossoms cover the plant summer through fall; attractive, fluffy seed heads then follow
the 2 in. blossoms. Prepare a fertile, well-drained soil, give
moderate watering, and grow in full sun or light shade.
As with most Clematis, shading the roots is very important.
Hardy to 0°. [7]

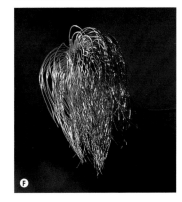

A *Clerodendrum bungei.* GLORY BOWER.
To 6 ft. (China)

Large, somewhat coarsely toothed leaves give a tropical
look to the garden. The deep green leaves support clusters
of purple-red flowers, which are held on terminal stalks.
Partially deciduous even in our mild climate. Can self-sow
in the garden. Plant in light shade to full sun on the coast
in rich, well-drained soils and give average water. Hardy
to about 20°. [3]

B *Coleonema pulchrum* 'Golden Sunset'
(*syn.* 'Sunset Gold'). GOLDEN BREATH
OF HEAVEN.
2 ft. (South Africa)

Coleonema has short and narow leaves. This cultivar has
striking golden foliage and a low-growing, horizontal habit.
Prune lightly after blooming to control size. Pale pink flowers
appear late winter and spring, with sporadic blossoms into
August. Drainage is important. Plant in full sun on the coast
to light shade inland in well-drained soil and supply moderate watering. The golden color is often of better quality in
light shade. Hardy to at least 20°. [4, 9]

C *Colocasia esculenta* 'Fontanesii'.
BLACK-STEM ELEPHANT'S EAR.
4–6 ft. (Tropical east Asia)

This selection of ELEPHANT'S EAR has purple-black
stems and large, dark greenish black leaves. The plants
grow from rhizomes and need regular watering and good
compost-enriched soil. Plant in light shade. Tropical-looking
ELEPHANT'S EAR is hardy to at least 25°. [3]

D *Convolvulus cneorum.* SILVERBUSH.

2–4 ft. (Southern Europe)

This showy shrub has silvery gray foliage and 2 in. white flowers that begin in late January and continue to summer. The brilliant white flowers rest atop the silver foliage and are better in light shade, where they can truly sparkle. Drainage is very important, as this plant is susceptible to crown and root rots, especially in the heat of summer. Often short-lived; one should add this to the list of plants used as annuals. The silver and white coloring is a must in the garden. Plant in full sun or light shade and supply moderate watering. Hardy to about 10–15°. [1, 2]

E *Convolvulus tricolor.*

DWARF MORNING GLORY.

10–15 in. (Portugal to Greece, North Africa)

Here is a plant you can use as a showstopper. Brilliant blue flowers with white and yellow in the throat draw everyone's attention. It is best to plant out young plants as they quickly get leggy in pots. Self-sows in the garden for future treats. Plant in full sun in well-drained soil and give moderate water. Hardy to about 15°. [8. 9]

Coprosma repens. MIRROR PLANT
(or LOOKING-GLASS PLANT).

(New Zealand)

MIRROR PLANTS are showy yet tough evergreen shrubs. They can tolerate some coastal exposure. Prune plants lightly one to two times a year to produce full-looking specimens. They tend to get leggy if left alone. Their shiny, rounded leaves give the plant its common names. Plant in full sun or light shade in well-drained soil and supply moderate watering. Hardy to about 25–30°.

F 'JIM DUGGAN'. 3–4 ft. My own selection from 'Marble Queen' with nearly pure white leaves. [4, 9]

G 'MARBLE QUEEN'. 3–4 ft. Glossy green leaves edged and marbled with white. [4]

H 'PINK SPLENDOR'. 3–4 ft. Shiny, dark green leaves heavily edged with yellow and tinged pink. [9]

Cordyline australis. GIANT DRACAENA
(or NEW ZEALAND CABBAGE PALM).

Leaves to 3 ft. (New Zealand)

In their youth these yucca-like plants form large crowns of
long narrow leaves. With time the crown rises on a narrow,
treelike stalk. Plant in full sun to light shade in well-drained
soil and supply only moderate watering, because Cordyline
will be quite drought-tolerant when established. Hardy to
about 18°.

A 'ALBERTII'. Green leaves brightly edged with a light
cream yellow, often tinged with a lovely pink color. [4]
B 'SUNDANCE'. Medium green leaves with light red center
stripe. [6]

C *Cornus alba* 'Spaethii'. GOLD-VARIEGATED
TARTARIAN DOGWOOD.

5–10 ft. (Siberia, northern China, and Korea)

Brilliant yellow-splashed leaves clothe this plant during
the growing season. When it loses its leaves in late fall,
colorful red stems appear. Probably best with some shade
and needing regular water; plant in well-drained soil. Hardy
to about 0°. [4]

Cornus stolonifera. RED OSIER DOGWOOD.

(North America)

Shrubby dogwoods are native to stream areas and can
spread by rhizomes or aboveground stolons to form large
colonies. Trim back the spreading roots to control size.
Conventional wisdom tells us that in Southern California
the leaves burn up during our hot summers. I find that with
regular watering these plants can be grown successfully
without burning. I have left several plants in the Central
Garden year-round and they have performed splendidly
without burning. Their great use, however, comes from their
brilliantly colored stems, which shine during winter. I use
them as winter annuals, removing them back to the nursery
during the warmer months. Plant them out in November as
they go deciduous for a striking winter garden. They need
good moisture and well-drained soil and will be best in light
shade in hotter areas. Hardy to about 0°.

'FLAVERIMEA'. GOLDEN TWIG DOGWOOD. To 10 ft. or more. This selection has yellow stems; new leaves appear in March followed by clusters of white flowers. [2, 4, 8, 9]
'ISANTI'. Compact selection to 5 ft. with bright red stems; does not leaf out until May. [3, 6, 8]

Ⓕ *Cosmos sulphureus* 'Sunny Orange-Red'.
COSMOS.

1–2 ft. (Mexico)

A bright orange summer annual, 'Sunny Orange-Red' is a key accent color for many areas of the garden. Obviously it works in the bright areas, but try it with purple and violet flowers and with gray-leaved plants. Robert Irwin uses 'Sunny Orange-Red' as the ideal "kicker" color in the lavender-flowered, midrange area of the Bowl. Plant in full sun in most soils and supply moderate watering. Can self-sow in the garden. Annual. [8]

Ⓖ *Crassula ovata* 'Tricolor'.
VARIEGATED JADE PLANT.

3–5 ft. (South Africa)

A showy landscape plant with green and white succulent leaves often tinged pink. White flowers appear in February and March. Very easy and tolerant of many growing conditions but best planted in full sun to light shade in well-drained soil with little water once established. Hardy to at least 27°. [1]

Ⓗ *Crinum asiaticum.*
RED ASIATIC POISON LILY.

3–4 ft. (Tropical Southeast Asia)

A superb deep red leaf form of this amaryllid with matching deep pink flowers. Flower stalks arise from large bulbs that form good-sized clumps. Plant in full sun to light shade in most soils with regular water. Hardy to about 20°. [3, 6, 8]

Cuphea hyssopifolia. FALSE HEATHER.

6 in. to 2 ft. (Central America)

Small perennial shrubs with narrow, ½ in.-long leaves carrying tiny flowers, which in warm areas fill the plants with near continuous bloom throughout the year. Plant in full sun to light shade in most soils and supply moderate watering. Cupheas tolerate considerable root competition and survive under trees and palms, where most plants will not. Hardy to about 25°.

Ⓐ 'ALLYSON PURPLE'. Glossy green leaves and purple flowers. [3]

Ⓑ 'AUREA'. GOLDEN FOLIAGE. Gold-green leaves with purple flowers. [4]

Ⓒ 'LAVENDER'. Excellent selection with medium purple flowers and somewhat darker leaves. [3, 8]

Ⓓ *Cupressus macrocarpa* 'Golden Pillar'.
GOLDEN MONTEREY CYPRESS.

To 16 ft. (Garden origin)

In time, MONTEREY CYPRESS can become a very large tree. I use this golden form in the garden and in pots when it is young. 'Golden Pillar' is slow-growing in youth and makes a bright statement in the garden. (Do not be afraid to use a plant for its moment; it really is OK.) When MONTEREY CYPRESSES get too large I replace them with younger plants. Best color is in full sun; shade tends to green the foliage up. Grow in full sun in well-drained soil and supply moderate water. Hardy to 15–20°. [9]

Dahlia. DAHLIA.

1½–5 ft. (Mexico, Central America, and Colombia) DAHLIAS are the keys to the summer garden; without them it just doesn't work. Grown from tubers planted in the spring, they produce nearly constant flowers all summer into fall. The tubers should be planted horizontally, 6 in. deep. Place a stake near the eye at planting, so you don't damage the tuber later on. Staking is necessary. I start plants for the Central Garden in pots and then put them in when they are about 12 in. high. This requires a small trick, because DAHLIAS do not form many fine lateral roots, which would hold the soil together when planting out. I line the sides of the pot with window screen to keep the soil and root mass from falling apart. The most problematic disease is powdery mildew. We spray the plants thoroughly (above and below the leaf) with refined horticultural oil, and doing this regularly keeps the leaf fresh and green. Hardy to about 15°.

E 'FASCINATION'. 1½–2 ft. Dark green foliage; deep lavender flowers. [6, 8]

F 'GITTS ATTENTION'. 3–4 ft. Creamy white. [7, 9]

G 'HIZZY FITZ'. 4 ft. Lacinated petals; bright yellow; sturdy stems. [9]

H 'RIP CITY'. 4 ft. Very deep red, nearly black. [6, 8]

I 'RIPPLES'. 4 ft. A sport of 'Rip City', velvety dark purple. [6, 8]

J 'SUNSTRUCK'. 4–4½ ft. Lacinated petals, bright yellow. [9]

K 'TANJOH'. 3½ ft. White tipped with deep fuchsia. [7, 8]

L 'WORTON'S BLUE STREAK'. 3 ft. Bluish lavender. [7, 8, 9]

A *Dalechampia dioscoreifolia*. PURPLE WINGS.
Vine (Costa Rica to Peru)
A unique and colorful vine with large oval leaves on slender twining stems. The color arrives with purple flower bracts that are the same size as the leaves. In the center of the flower bracts is an extraordinary glossy black sphere with distinct markings that resemble a face. Visitors to the garden always comment on this beautiful vine with the smiling face. Color begins in spring with a peak in summer and sporadic bracts into late fall and early winter. Plant in full sun with good drainage and give average water to produce a moderately sized vine that produces flower bracts throughout most of the year. Hardy to at least 27°. [8]

B *Deschampsia cespitosa* 'Northern Lights'.
VARIEGATED HAIRGRASS.
6–8 in. (North America, Eurasia)
Tight clumps of narrow leaves brightly striped with creamy white. One fun combination we used was to combine this with clumps of BLACK MONDO GRASS, each making the other a more attractive plant. 'Northern Lights' tends to revert to green, so keep a watchful eye and remove the green leaves. Plant in light shade or full sun in most soils and give moderate water. Hardy to 10° or less. [2, 7]

C *Dianella tasmanica*. FLAX LILY.
3–5 ft. (Southeastern Australia, including Tasmania)
An evergreen perennial with sword-shaped leaves that are deep green in color. Small blue flowers begin to appear in spring on erect stalks and are followed in summer by pendent, bright, metallic blue berries. There are two variegated forms of the FLAX LILY, with the leaves striped either with yellow or with white. Best in light shade but can take sun in coastal areas. Tolerates most soils and takes moderate watering. Hardy to about 18°. [3]

D 'BLUSHY'. This selection has leaves broadly striped with white and some pink tones. [2, 7]

❺ *Dianthus* 'Black and White Minstrels'. PINK.
To 1 ft. (Garden origin)

An evergreen perennial with narrow leaves and flowers having deep purple-black centers fading to red-purple with
white tips. Peak flowering comes in spring, with occasional
blossoms at other times. Best planted in full sun and with
good drainage and receiving moderate water. Prune after
blooming to keep compact. Hardy to about 0°. [9]

❻ *Diascia* 'Ice Cracker'. TWINSPUR.
(South Africa)

TWINSPUR is a small-scale perennial that, although short-
lived, should find its way into all gardens. Nearly constant
flowering makes this a superb filler. Thin stems are clothed
in narrow, gray-green leaves. Shear off old flowers for
longer life and more bloom. Diascia can spread by underground stems to form good-sized colonies. They do best in
full sun to light shade with good drainage and average
water. Hardy to about 20°. [7, 8]

❼ *Dietes* 'Orange Drop'. FORTNIGHT LILY.
2 ft. (South Africa)

This selection is somewhat smaller growing than Dietes irid-
ioides and carries cream-colored, IRIS-like flowers with a
distinctive orange blotch. Peak flowering is spring to summer with occasional blossoms nearly year-round. The clumping leaves are narrow and deep green. Extremely tough and
resilient plant that will grow in many situations from sun to
light shade in most soils with moderate watering. Hardy to
about 15–20°. [3]

ⓐ *Dudleya pulverulenta.* CHALK LETTUCE.
To 2 ft. (Southwestern United States and north-western Mexico)

Striking, succulent rosettes with silver-gray leaves. Flower stalks appear from March to July. Plant in full sun to light shade in well-drained soil with moderate watering during the winter and spring growing season and much less during summer. Plants shine during the growing season but will look a bit ratty during late summer. Planting the rosette at an angle to keep water out of the crown helps in less than ideal locations. Hardy to about 20°. [2]

ⓑ *Dymondia margaretae.*
1–2 in. (South Africa)

Dymondia is a very tough, drought-tolerant ground cover with silvery-green leaves. This mat-forming perennial can tolerate light foot traffic. Best in drier areas, as it is a little aggressive with a lot of water. Stemless yellow daisy flowers in warm months. Plant in full sun or light shade and supply moderate watering. Hardy to about 20°. [5]

Echeveria. ECHEVERIA.
(Texas, Mexico, Central America to Andes)

A large group of succulents that form fleshy rosettes. There is a huge variety of colorful shadings and leaf shapes. Thick-stemmed flower stalks emerge from between the leaves and carry drooping flowers. I often cut the flower stems out, as the rosette looks better by itself. Plant in full sun on the coast to light shade elsewhere in a very well-drained soil and supply only moderate watering. Hardy to about 20°.

ⓒ 'AFTERGLOW'. Large wide leaves, soft reddish lavender rosettes. [1]
ⓓ 'DONDO'. Yellow-green rosettes, orange flowers. [1]
ⓔ 'DORIS TAYLOR'. Hairy green rosettes, orange flowers. [1]
ⓕ 'LOLA'. Perfect 3–4 in. rosettes, pearl-white with pink-gray tinge. [1, 2]
ⓖ 'PERLE VON NURNBERG'. Large wide leaves, pearl-lavender flowers. [1]
ⓗ *SUBSESSILIS.* Smaller leaves and rosettes, leaves blue-gray. [1, 2]

Echinacea purpurea. CONEFLOWER
(or ECHINACEA).

   3–4 ft. (Eastern United States)

CONEFLOWERS are perennials that form large basal
clumps of deep green leaves. Late spring through summer
brings tall stalks of large, showy, daisylike flowers with
reflexed rays. Planting in full sun in most soils and supplying
average water will produce lush plants. CONEFLOWER is
winter-deciduous but comes back in March with new
growth. Hardy to at least 0°.

Ⓘ 'BRAVADO'. Purple flowers. [8]
Ⓙ 'MAGNUS'. Reddish purple flowers to 7 in. wide. [8]
Ⓚ 'WHITE SWAN'. White flowers. [8]

Ⓛ *Echium vulgare* 'Blue Bedder'. BLUEWEED.

   12–15 in. (Europe)

'Blue Bedder' is an annual that freely reseeds in the garden. Beautiful, clear blue flowers appear early and last for
some months. The light green foliage is somewhat hairy.
Can be sown nearly any time of the year for quick bloom in
coastal areas. Best in full sun in most soils and with moderate water. Hardy to at least 20°. [7]

Ⓜ *Equisetum scirpoides.* DWARF HORSETAIL.

   6 in. (North America)

DWARF HORSETAIL enjoys lots of moisture and resembles
a small tufted cleaning brush. The jointed stems are very
dark green and form vigorous spreading clumps. Be careful
where you plant DWARF HORSETAIL, as it can be difficult
to remove when established. Grow in full sun or light shade
in moisture-retentive soil. Hardy to about 10°. [5]

Ⓐ *Erodium × variabile* 'Album'. STORKSBILL.
3 in. × 12 in. (Temperate America, Eurasia, North Africa, Australia)
Erodiums are evergreen perennial ground covers that are sprinkled with ½ in. flowers throughout the year. This selection has white flowers. Plant in full sun on the coast to light shade inland in well-drained soil and supply moderate watering. These plants have a very long and steady blooming period. Hardy to about 15°. [2]

Ⓑ *Eryngium* 'Sapphire Blue'.
BLUE-STEM SEA HOLLY.
1½ –2 ft. (Garden origin)
In my travels I came across this spectacular hybrid SEA HOLLY. I had only one plant, and since it is patented I could not make more. Bob Irwin was visiting my nursery and stumbled on my lone selection. "Why isn't this in the garden? Are you holding out on me?" It took another year, but finally the plant was available from wholesalers. BLUE-STEM SEA HOLLY has bright blue stems and flower heads. It really draws your attention. Plant in full sun to light shade in well-drained soil and give moderate watering. Hardy to about 15°. [2, 7]

Ⓒ *Eryngium maritimum.* SEA HOLLY.
1½ ft. (Europe)
This species has stiff, blue-gray leaves with spiny edges. The thistlelike flowers are a similar blue-gray in color. The growth habit is mounding and looks good spilling over a wall. Plant in full sun in well-drained soils and give moderate watering. Hardy to about 10°. [7]

D *Eryngium variifolium.*
MOROCCAN SEA HOLLY.
1½–2 ft. (Morocco)

A very ornamental SEA HOLLY with smaller rosettes of deep green leaves that are lined with white. The attractive flower stalks carry striking silver flowers and begin in June and last into late summer. Plant in full sun in well-drained soils and give moderate watering. Hardy to about 10°. [7]

E *Erysimum* 'Bowles' Mauve.'
SHRUBBY WALLFLOWER.
3 ft. (Garden origin)

Superb shrubby perennial that forms a rounded mound with gray-green leaves and delicate stalks of purple flowers. The flower stalks begin in late winter and early spring and slowly elongate with the nearly perpetual blooms. 'Bowles Mauve' can be short-lived because of its tendency to "bloom itself to death." Best planted in full sun to light shade in a well-drained soil and given only moderate water. Hardy to about 15°. [1, 2]

F *Eschscholzia californica.*
CALIFORNIA POPPY.
1½–2 ft. (Western North America)

A key accent color in gray or blue-gray areas for Irwin is orange. This becomes a "kicker" color that activates the gray-toned plants, pushing them in one direction or the other. CALIFORNIA POPPY is an ideal choice for a bright orange. This is actually a perennial that is often grown as an annual. Finely divided blue-green leaves hold the glowing flowers. Grow in full sun or light shade in well-drained soils and supply moderate water. Quite hardy. [1, 2]

G *MARITIMA.* 8–10 in. I really like this plant. It resembles a small-scale CALIFORNIA POPPY but with softer yellow-orange flowers. [2]

Ⓐ *Euphorbia characias* subsp. *wulfenii.*
MEDITERRANEAN SPURGE.

3–4 ft. (Southern Europe)

A very tough perennial with blue-green leaves; it grows into an upright, rounded bush and sports large heads of chartreuse-colored flower clusters that begin in midwinter, reaching a striking peak from March to June. Plant in full sun to light shade and give reasonably good drainage with moderate watering. Initial transplanting can sometimes be a problem, with established plants reseeding in the garden. Hardy to about 10°. [2]

Ⓑ *Euphorbia cotinifolia.* COPPER TREE.

12–15 ft. (Mexico and northern South America)

COPPER TREE is a beautiful accent plant for the garden, with truly ornamental, deep red leaves and a shiny smooth bark. Deciduous in the winter months when the smooth bark is at its best. Plant in full sun to light shade in a well-drained soil and supply moderate watering. Hardy to about 27°. [7, 9]

Ⓒ *Euphorbia dulcis* 'Chameleon.'
DWARF PURPLE SPURGE.

1½ ft. (Western Europe to Macedonia)

New foliage is a deep red that can green up in time, giving this selection the color-changing name of 'Chameleon'. Flowers are also a deep red and persist for some time. Often difficult to transplant, they will, however, occasionally reseed. Plant in full sun in well-drained soil with average water. Hardy to about 10°. [4, 9]

❶ *Euphorbia rigida.* SPURGE.

2 ft. (Morocco, Mediterranean, Iran)

This clumping perennial has 2 ft.-long, snakelike branches covered with blue-green leaves. Chartreuse-green flowers are borne on terminal tips in late winter and spring. Remove old woody stems after new growth is about 4–6 in. long. Plant in full sun to light shade in a well-drained soil and give moderate water. Hardy to at least 27°. [1, 7]

❷ *Euphorbia tirucallii* 'Sticks of Fire'.
PENCIL TREE.

2–4 ft. (Tropical and southern Africa)

This brilliant selection is smaller than the species and has yellow-orange stems with deep orange tips. A valuable accent plant especially when backlit by the sun. Plant in full sun with good drainage and supply moderate watering. Plants go through a dormant phase in midsummer and lose some of their coloring, but new growth soon follows that brings back the wonderfully brilliant color. Hardy to at least 27°. [1, 4, 7]

❸ *Fallopia japonica* 'Variegata'.
VARIEGATED FALLOPIA.

To 4 ft. (Japan)

Here is another showstopping plant. This woody perennial has brilliant white variegated leaves lightly touched with pink that cover the plant during the growing season. Deciduous in winter, but well worth the wait, as the new growth is striking. This is a vigorous spreader, so keep your eye open. Hardy to about –15°. [2]

Farfugium japonicum.
To 2 ft. (Eastern Asia)

A small genus of two species of rhizomatous perennials with large leathery leaves. Clusters of 1–2 in. flower heads on stiff stalks begin in the fall, an added bonus because many other summer plants are over. They perform best in light shade to full shade but will take some sun along the coast (especially morning sun). Plant in compost-enriched, well-drained soil and give regular water. Roots hardy to about 0°.

Ⓐ 'ARGENTEUM'. Leaves heavily blotched with irregular patches of creamy white. [2]
Ⓑ 'CRISPATUM'. Very showy grayish yellow-green leaves that are fantastically crested and wavy. [2]

Ⓒ *Felicia amelloides* 'Variegata'.
VARIEGATED BLUE MARGUERITE.
1½–2 ft.

A beautiful selection of BLUE MARGUERITE with leaves heavily splashed with white and having blue with yellow-centered, asterlike flowers throughout much of the year. Tolerant of most soils but does poorly in wet areas. Plant in full sun and give average water. Hardy to at least 27°. [4, 9]

Festuca. FESCUE.
(Europe)

Ornamental grasses with narrow leaves and which form dense rounded mounds. Attractive, airy flower stalks appear in spring and last into June, with attractive tan seed heads persisting into early summer. Good drainage is essential for success. Plant in full sun to light shade in a well-drained soil and give moderate watering. Hardy to about 10°.

Ⓓ *MUELLERI.* **'MUELLER'S FESCUE'.** 8–12 in. (New South Wales and Victoria, Australia). Fine, hairlike green leaves. [3]
Ⓔ 'SISKIYOU BLUE'. 1 ft. Blue-gray foliage. [2]

❻ *Fuchsia procumbens.* TRAILING FUCHSIA.
   6 in. (New Zealand)
Rich green heart-shaped leaves on a somewhat vining,
prostrate plant. Large showy red berries follow small flowers. Plant in light shade in good compost-enriched soil and
supply regular water. Protect from frost. [3]

❼ *Fuchsia thymifolia* 'Variegata.'
VARIEGATED THYME-LEAVED FUCHSIA.
   2–4 ft. (Mexico)
Small, half-inch leaves heavily splashed with creamy white
with a pink tinge. Growth starts out with a prostrate habit
but soon erect stems emerge, creating a spreading shrub.
Best in light shade in good compost-enriched soil with regular water. Protect from frost. Hardy to about 20°. [2, 3]

Fuchsia triphylla. SHRUBBY FUCHSIA.
   3–4 ft. (Hispaniola)
One of the more sun-tolerant FUCHSIAS with a nearly perpetual blooming habit. Drooping clusters of orange-red
tubular flowers cover these shrubby specimens. Plant in full
sun to light shade (especially in very warm areas) in good
compost-enriched soil and supply regular water. Takes heat
better than most but is hurt by frost. Hardy to at least 25°.

❽ 'FIRECRACKER' (Garden origin). A new hybrid with
leaves heavily splashed with white and striped with red and
green. The flower clusters are pendent and orange-red.
Plant in light shade in compost-enriched soil and give regular water. Damaged by frost. [2]

❾ 'GARTENMEISTER BONSTEDT' (West Indian hybrid).
Leaves are a deep green with a purple underside. [6]

Gaura lindheimeri. WHITE GAURA.

1–1½ ft. (Southern United States)

One of the easiest perennials for our gardens, with numerous stems lined with butterflylike flowers. Blooms begin in spring and flush heavily into summer when it is best to cut plants back for a second flowering later in fall. Prune again in early spring for the new year's bloom cycle. Some forms are almost too easy, as they can reseed prolifically. Plant in full sun in well-drained soil and give only moderate water. Very drought-tolerant when established but will also take water. Hardy to at least 0°.

A **'CORRIE'S GOLD'.** A variegated selection with light yellow, white, and green leaves; white flowers. [9]
B **'SISKIYOU PINK'.** Deep green leaves with reddish tints, pink flowers; blooms a little earlier than 'Corrie's Gold'. [3, 9]

C *Gazania* 'Trailing White'. GAZANIA.

8 in. (South Africa)

Perennial ground cover (there are annuals as well) with silver-gray leaves and white, daisylike flowers. GAZANIAS are versatile fillers but many are short-lived, succumbing to dieback. I have found two (this one and 'Mitsua Yellow') that are very sturdy, lasting well in the garden. Tolerant of most soils; plant in full sun to light shade and give only moderate watering. Hardy to about 15°. [2]

Geranium. CRANESBILL.
Mounding to spreading perennials with leaves that are
often deeply cut or lobed. The more prolific growers can
be cut back in November to control size. Plant in full sun
to light shade in a well-drained soil and supply moderate
watering. Hardy to at least 10°.

D 'ANN FOLKARD'. 1 × 2 ft. (Garden origin). Amazing
selection with yellow-green variegated leaves; flowers are a
rich magenta with a black eye 1¼ in. in size and are present
spring to late fall; leaves keep their color throughout our
summer heat; a strong grower with long, twining stems. [9]

E *HARVEYI.* 1 ft. (South Africa). Beautiful silvery leaves add
striking color to the garden; flowers are light violet; plants
spread quickly and can reseed. [2, 7]

F 'PHILIPPE VAPELLE'. 15 in. (Garden origin). Richly textured, deep green leaves; 1½ in. blue-purple flowers with
dark veins begin in February. A superior selection, as it
burns only slightly in our summer heat. [8]

G 'STANHOE'. 10 in. × 24 in. (Garden origin). Small-scale
ground cover with gray-green leaves and nearly everblooming pale pink flowers; a very easy plant. [2]

H *Geranium maderense.*
3–3½ ft. (Madeira)
The largest of the true geraniums with large, glossy green
leaves to 1 ft. across that are strongly palmately divided.
A short-lived perennial that often flowers in its second year
with hundreds of light purple flowers that form a dome over
the leaves in spring. The mother plant will die after flowering, but pups will usually form at the base and volunteers
frequently spring up nearby. A tremendous accent plant
that is best in light shade. Do not cut away old leaf stems,
because they support the top-heavy flower cluster. Plant
in a well-drained soil and give average watering. Hardy to
about 20°. [3, 4, 8]

Ⓐ *Glaucium flavum.*
YELLOW HORNED POPPY.
1 ft. (Europe, Canary Islands)

This is a fantastic gray-leaved perennial that does well in partial shade. Because gray coloring is often a plant defense against the sun, it's tough to find good gray plants for shady areas. The YELLOW HORNED POPPY has glaucous, heavily ruffled, and deeply lobed leaves with yellow (sometimes orange), poppylike flowers. They rarely flower here at the Getty, but the stunning leaves, which form lush rosettes, offer more than enough interest. These perennials can be short-lived. They enjoy excellent drainage and prefer partial shade. Hardy to about 15°. [2, 7]

Ⓑ *Haloragis erectus* 'Wellington Bronze'.
2–3 ft. (New Zealand)

'Wellington Bronze' is a unique accent plant with slender, dark bronze leaves on a fast-growing perennial. Its final size belies the somewhat dainty look of the young plant. Plant in full sun in well-drained soil and give moderate water. Can self-sow in the garden. Hardy to 20–25°. [6]

Hebe. HEBE.
2–3 ft. (New Zealand)

HEBES are beautiful accent shrubs with dense flower clusters that appear in late spring and into summer. Shear off old flowers but keep any major pruning to a minimum; never prune into old wood. Good garden soil that is well drained with regular water is needed for healthy plants. Plants can occasionally be short-lived because of fungal and root problems. HEBES will take the sun on the coast but seem happier in light shade. Hardy to about 18°.

Ⓒ 'AMY'. 2–3 ft. Purple-tinged new leaves and violet flower spikes. [3, 8]

Ⓓ 'MCKEANII'. Tight mounds of deep green foliage; leaves resemble conifer scales. [3]

Ⓔ *PIMELEOIDES* 'QUICKSILVER'. 1½ ft. Small silver-gray leaves, dark stems. [2]

Helenium autumnale. SNEEZEWEED.

(Canada, eastern United States)

Old-fashioned tough perennial that grows from a slowly spreading crown and carries daisylike flowers atop an erect stem in late summer. Deadhead for more continuous bloom. Valued in the garden for its late summer and fall blossoms. It needs full sun and good, well-drained soil with moderate water. Hardy to at least 0°.

F 'MOERHEIM BEAUTY'. Moderately sized at 2–3 ft. with deep orange flowers. [9]

G 'ROTGOLD'. Yellow and golden-red flowers on 2½–3 ft. stems. [9]

H 'SUNSHINE'. Tall growing, to 4–5 ft., with bright yellow flowers. [9]

I *Helichrysum* 'Icicles'. STRAWFLOWERS.

1 ft. (Garden origin)

A wonderful accent plant with narrow, silvery leaves and yellow flowers that are best sheared off as they detract from the silvery foliage. Plant in full sun in well-drained soil and supply moderate water. Hardy to about 20°. [1]

J *Heliotropium arborescens* 'Black Beauty'. HELIOTROPE.

15–36 in. (Peru)

Wonderful semierect perennial with deep purple-tinged leaves and purple-black flowers that have a very special fragrance. A very long bloom period, spring to fall, makes this a treasure for the garden. HELIOTROPE often looks poor during the cooler winter months but comes back well in early spring. Feed plants regularly before cool weather arrives and continue to help them through winter. (Some growers will cut plants back sharply in winter to force a rest period.) Can be grown in full sun on the coast but is probably best in light shade elsewhere. HELIOTROPE needs a good garden soil and excellent drainage with average water to perform well. Hardy to about 25–30°. [3, 4, 8]

Helleborus. HELLEBORE.

2–3 ft. (Southern Europe)

These old-fashioned garden favorites are lovely, undemanding perennials. They carry clusters of flowers beginning in late December and persisting throughout winter and early spring. Although HELLEBORES will take full sun on the coast, I find that light shade is preferable in most cases. Plant in a well-drained soil and supply moderate watering. Hardy to about 0°.

Ⓐ *ARGUTIFOLIUS*. CORSICAN HELLEBORE. Large, blue-green leaves that are heavily serrated, heavy clusters of light chartreuse flowers; self-sows in the garden. [3, 7, 8]

Ⓑ *ARGUTIFOLIUS* 'JANET STARNES'. Showy, variegated leaves. [1, 2, 7]

Ⓒ *FOETIDUS* 'CHEDGLOW'. Spectacular chartreuse leaves, strongly divided leaflets. [2]

Ⓓ *FOETIDUS* 'RED SILVER'. Steel-gray leaves, strongly divided leaflets. [2]

Ⓔ *ORIENTALIS* 'CONCORD'. Deep purple-black flowers. [2]

Ⓕ *ORIENTALIS* 'SLATE'. Slate-black flowers. [2]

Ⓖ *Hemerocallis* 'Red Tet'. DAYLILY.

18 inches, with flowers to 2½ ft. (Garden origin)

DAYLILIES are stalwart perennials of the garden, forming clumps of long, strapped-shaped leaves. Because they rarely suffer from disease, are easy to grow, and are tolerant of many different garden conditions, they are a must for the garden. 'Red Tet' is a rich red with a yellow center, begins flowering in late spring, and persists throughout the warmer summer months. Each flower only lasts a day, but more are produced in quick succession. Plant in full sun or light shade in most soils and supply moderate watering. Hardy to at least 0°. [6]

Ⓗ *Hibiscus trionum.* FLOWER-OF-AN-HOUR.
   To 2 ft. (Probably from Australia)
A low-growing, ground-cover Hibiscus with deep green, deeply lobed leaves and attractive 3 in. white flowers with dark centers that are followed by light brown, papery seed pods. The bloom period is long, spring to summer. Trim back the long runners for compactness. In mild climates it can be perennial and can self-sow in the garden. Plant in full sun in well-drained soil and supply moderate water. Hardy to about 27–30°. [8]

Ⓘ *Hunnemannia fumariifolia.*
MEXICAN TULIP POPPY.
   2–3 ft. (Mexico)
Brilliant, clear yellow flowers from late spring through fall on finely divided blue-green foliage. MEXICAN TULIP POPPY forms soft, bushy plants that add grace to the garden. Sometimes difficult to start from pots but reliably reseeds in the garden. Seed best sown in late winter directly into garden. Plant in full sun or light shade in a well-drained soil and supply moderate watering. Hardy to about 15–20°. [2]

Hydrangea macrophylla.
BIG-LEAF HYDRANGEA.
   (Japan, Korea)
Rounded shrubs with large, bright green leaves. These selections, the 'Lace-Cap' varieties, have flattened flower clusters of small sterile white flowers surrounded by a ring of larger pink flowers. Flower buds begin to form in spring, with peak flowering in early summer. Flower color is dictated by pH. In our alkaline soils blossoms will be pink, and in acid soils they will be blue. HYDRANGEAS need a good soil, enriched with compost, and a regular supply of water. After flowering prune hard to outside buds to create a compact plant. Old canes should be removed occasionally to encourage a fresher plant. In cooler climates plants can be deciduous. Full sun on the coast to light shade inland. Hardy to about 0°.

Ⓙ 'MARIESII'. 4–8 ft. Rich green leaves; watch for mildew. [3]
Ⓚ 'VEITCHII'. 3–5 ft. White-flower variety. [3]

Ipomoea batatas. SWEET POTATO.

(Pantropical)

The SWEET POTATO is a favorite food for many, and these ornamentally leaved varieties make a great splash in the garden. They will be deciduous in the cold of winter, but spring brings forth vigorous growing vines clothed in deeply lobed leaves. I use this as the ultimate ground cover under DAHLIAS. As the summer season runs on, the DAHLIAS tend to get bare stems at their base, and these lush SWEET POTATO leaves solve the problem. One initial tuber quickly increases during the growing season. I divide them in winter, giving me many new plants for the next season. Plant in full sun in well-drained soil and give regular water. Cut down by frosts; likes a warm location. Hardy to at least 25°.

Ⓐ 'BLACKIE'. Deeply lobed purple-black leaves with purple stems. [8]

Ⓑ 'MARGARITA'. Golden-yellow-chartreuse leaves. [9]

Ⓒ *Ipomoea lobata.* SPANISH FLAG.

Vine (Mexico, Central America, and South America)

SPANISH FLAG is a short-lived perennial treated as a warm-weather annual, with remarkable flowers colored yellow and red-orange. Sow seeds as early as possible. Even in Southern California, if spring is cool the plants do not do well. Needs a long warm period to put on the best show. Plant in full sun in well-drained soil and give regular water. [9]

Ipomoea purpurea.
COMMON MORNING GLORY.

Vine (Mexico)

During the summer it's always fun to cover a trellis with the heart-shaped leaves of this annual MORNING GLORY. There is a wide range of flower colors from white to red to blue. True to their names, the flowers open mainly in the morning. Plant in full sun to light shade in most soils and give moderate water. Annual.

Ⓓ 'HEAVENLY BLUE'. Sky-blue flowers with a white throat. [8]

Ⓔ 'SCARLETT O'HARA'. Rich red flowers with a white throat. [8]

Iris. DUTCH IRIS.

2 ft. (Spain, Portugal, Sicily, Northern Africa)

DUTCH IRISES are some of the easiest and most reliable bulbs for spring flowering in Southern California. They do not need to be chilled or lifted when dormant. Plant them out and watch them get better year after year. Plant bulbs in the fall, 4–5 in. deep in well-drained soil and give average water during the growing season. Allow the foliage to ripen to build up strength for next year. Very hardy but mulch in cold areas.

F 'BLUE RIBBON'. Blue with a yellow mark on the falls. [8]
G 'RUSTY BEAUTY'. Robert Irwin's favorite; a rusty orange with brownish falls. [9]
H 'SAPPHIRE BEAUTY'. Purple with a yellow stripe. [6, 8]
I 'WHITE WEDGEWOOD'. White with a yellow mark on each fall. [7, 9]

J *Isoplexis canariensis.*

3 ft. (Tenerife)

It's difficult to find good orange-flowered shrubs, but this one really stands out. It resembles a bushy FOXGLOVE with terminal racemes of soft orange flowers. The leaves are deep green and leathery. Prune after flowering for compactness. Good drainage is very important. Grow in full sun in compost-enriched soil, and give regular watering. Hardy to about 28°. [9]

K *Isopogon formosus.* ROSE CONE FLOWER.

5–6 ft. (Australia)

An erect shrub clothed with much divided green leaves. Flower buds are very ornamental and last on the plant for many months; these are followed in late spring with purple-rose pincushion flowers on terminal growth. Prune after flowering for a more compact plant. Plant in full sun to light shade in a well-drained soil with moderate watering. Plants seem to fare better in light shade in our hotter areas. Hardy to about 18°. [2]

Ixia. CORN LILY.
7–25 in. (South Africa)

Ixia are winter- and spring-growing bulbs (actually corms) from South Africa. During the summer they are dormant and enjoy a dry rest period. Plant corms 2–3 in. deep in well-drained soil with full sun or light shade. During the growing season they enjoy regular moisture, but keep them dry during dormancy. Hardy to at least 27°.

Ⓐ *FLEXUOSA.* 13–18 in. Lightly fragrant with light pink flowers and yellow stamens. [3]

Ⓑ *MACULATA.* 11–16 in. Floriferous species with brilliant yellow-orange flowers accented with black centers. [4]

Ⓒ *VIRIDIFLORA.* 24–39 in. One of the most sought-after flowers from South Africa; light turquoise-green marked with purple-black centers; use a sand base as this one has a tendency to rot. [2, 7]

Ⓓ *Kalanchoe pumila.* KALANCHOE.
1 ft. (Madagascar)

This very easy and rewarding succulent has rounded gray leaves that support pink flowers late winter and spring. The coolness of winter brings a reddish pink hue to the leaves. Plant in full sun to light shade with good drainage and only moderate watering once established. Hardy to at least 27°. [1]

Ⓔ *Kalanchoe thyrsiflora.* KALANCHOE.
8–12 in. to 3 ft. in flower (South Africa)

Large (3–4 in.) roundish leaves colored a medium green and edged with red make this a great accent plant. During winter the leaves become even more suffused with red. This season also brings tall, slender flower stalks with small white flowers. Plant in full sun to light shade in well-drained soil and give only moderate watering. Hardy to at least 27°. [1]

❻ *Kniphofia* 'Gold Mine.' TORCH LILY
(or RED-HOT POKER).

Flowers to 2 ft. (South Africa)

Tough perennials that form rosettes of arching, narrow, pointed leaves. Flowering begins in April and continues sporadically throughout the year, mainly in summer, with rich orange flowers. Remove faded flowers for more bloom and cut old leaves off at base. The foliage looks a little tattered in late fall and can be pruned back during winter. Fresh leaves appear in spring. When planting set the crowns slightly high to avoid rots. Plant in full sun, in most soils and supply moderate water, with little water once established. Hardy to about 15°. [9]

❼ *Lagerstroemia indica* 'Muskogee.'
CRAPE MYRTLE.

To 25 in. (China)

CRAPE MYRTLE is a deciduous tree with lovely, exfoliating bark and profuse flowering in summer. As the smooth gray bark flakes off it reveals a lighter, almost pink coloring. The biggest problem with these trees, especially near the coast, is mildew. 'Muskogee' has been fairly mildew-resistant for us, but it does suffer a little. The lavender flowers are formed on new terminal shoots. Prune during dormancy to increase next year's flowering wood. We have had two flowerings each year in the Central Garden: one in early summer, usually July, and then an even more floriferous show in late summer or early fall, flushing in September. Plant in full sun in the warmest location, in most soils, and supply moderate water. [SURROUNDING THE BOWL GARDEN]

❽ *Lathyrus odoratus.* SWEET PEA.

Annual vine (Italian peninsula and Sicily)

A garden without SWEET PEAS in the spring just doesn't feel complete; the lovely colors and sweet fragrance make them a must. Before sowing soak the seeds in warm water for twenty-four hours. For the earliest bloom in Southern California start seeds in September; this can bring flowers for Christmas. When the weather is too cool, making the soil cold; seeds tend to rot more easily. Powdery mildew is the biggest problem, and this can be held off with regular sprays of refined horticultural oil. Plant in full sun in well-drained soil and give average water. Annual. [8, 9]

Lavandula. LAVENDER.

2–3 in. (Canary Islands, Mediterranean, northeastern Africa)

LAVENDERS are fragrant perennials that add a truly Mediterranean look to any garden. Many tend to be short-lived due to their dislike of poor drainage. The varieties listed below have proved to be much more tolerant of regular irrigation. These varieties also accept pruning better than most, but as a rule it is better to prune LAVENDERS lightly—only into newer growth. The bloom period is very long, often from February to July and August. Shear off old flowers to groom plants. Plant in full sun to light shade in a very well-drained soil and give only moderate watering. LAVENDERS seem to have a longer life under drier and somewhat sterile conditions. Hardy to about 20°.

Ⓐ × *HETEROPHYLLA* 'GOODWIN CREEK'. 2–3 ft. Garden hybrid with lush silver-gray leaves, a compact, rounded growth, and nearly continuous rich purple flower stalks that are held well above the foliage. [1, 2, 7]

Ⓑ × *INTERMEDIA* 'WALBERTONS'S SILVER EDGE'. 3–4 ft. Pale gray-green leaves with cream edges; lavender-violet flowers. [7]

Ⓒ *PINNATA*. JAGGED LAVENDER. 3–4 ft. Fine-textured, gray-green, lacy leaves with nearly year-round purple flowers on long stems; takes hard pruning better than other species. [8]

Ⓓ *Leucanthemum × superbum* 'Esther Read'. SHASTA DAISY.

To 2 ft. (Garden origin)

'Esther Read' is a tough, reliable perennial for the cut-flower garden. SHASTA DAISY can be long-lived but needs dividing every 2–3 years, when the old central crown is discarded. A long blooming period, spring through fall, makes this tough perennial a must. Cut out faded flower stems for more bloom. Plant in full sun in most soils and supply regular watering. Hardy to at least 20–25°. [7, 9]

❷ *Libertia peregrinans.*
GOLD-LEAF NEW ZEALAND IRIS.
1–1½ ft. (New Zealand)

IRIS-like herbaceous perennial with stiff, sword-shaped leaves colored orange with a central green rib. Spreads by underground rhizomes to form loose clusters of individual clumps. Small, ½ in. white flowers nestle among the leaves in spring and sporadically from summer to fall. Plant in full sun on the coast to light shade inland in a well-drained soil and give moderate water. Hardy to about 15°. [1, 4, 6, 9]

❸ *Lilium* 'Enchantment'. LILY.
20–24 in. (Garden origin)

Potted LILIES are popular gifts at Easter; 'Enchantment' is an Asiatic type with bright orange flowers. For Southern California gardens, most LILIES are really only good for one year. Their culture requires a very well-drained soil with the roots kept cool and in the shade. Supply regular moisture, because these bulbs do not like to dry out. Full sun on the coast to light shade inland. When buying bulbs, choose ones that are large and firm. In our warm climate the bulbs tend to get smaller with each year of growth. I like to buy new bulbs each year. LILIES are very hardy. [4, 9]

❹ *Limnanthes douglasii* subsp. *sulphurea.*
POINT REYES MEADOW FOAM.
2–4 in. (Oregon, California)

MEADOW FOAM is a cool-season annual native to California. This selection carries masses of 1 in., cup-shaped yellow flowers (the species has white tips on the petals). It offers a bright display atop the bright green leaves. Once you have planted this California native, it will self- seed in the garden, coming back year after year. Plant in full sun in well-drained soil and give regular moisture. [9]

A *Limonium psilocladium.* DWARF STATICE (or DWARF SEA-LAVENDER)

6–8 in. (Canary Islands)

DWARF STATICE has tight rosettes of rounded leaves and airy sprays of light violet flowers in late spring and summer. In its native habitat it is dormant and deciduous in summer. STATICES are some of the easiest perennials for Southern California gardens, often self-sowing in crevices and other unplanned areas. Plants are best in full sun with good drainage and moderate watering. Very drought-tolerant once established. Hardy to about 25°. [1, 2, 5]

B *Linaria purpurea* 'Natalie.' PURPLE TOADFLAX.

2–3 in. (Southern Europe)

A wonderful but sometimes short-lived perennial with narrow blue-gray leaves. 'Natalie' carries spikes of striking blue-purple snapdragon-like flowers in late spring and summer and sporadically into fall. TOADFLAX can self-sow in the garden. Plant in full sun to light shade in most soils and give moderate water. Hardy to about 15°. [7]

C *Linaria reticulata* 'Flamenco.'

8–12 in. (North Africa)

'Flamenco' is an annual Linaria with yellow and maroon flowers. It attracts everybody's attention. In coastal areas the seeds can be sown year-round to produce recurrent crops. Reseeding in the garden is an added treat. Plant in full sun in well-drained soil and give regular water. If old flowers are cut back, the flowering season can be extended. [9]

◑ *Lobelia erinus* 'Crystal Palace'. LOBELIA.
   6 in. (South Africa)

Everyone is familiar with LOBELIAS; they seem to be in
everyone's garden. 'Crystal Palace' is a great surprise
color for nearly every section. Robert Irwin likes to use just
a few plants, nestled in small niches in unexpected areas.
Whenever it self-sows the "accidents" produced are usually
better than those planned. Apparently it is a perennial, but
it is treated as an annual. [1, 7]

◑ *Lobelia* 'Queen Victoria'.
PERENNIAL LOBELIA.
   1½–2 ft. (Garden origin)

'Queen Victoria' forms tight, slowly spreading clumps of
purple-red leaves. Tall spikes of red flowers appear late
spring and summer. The main flower spike will send off
smaller auxiliary stems, so deadhead only the faded sections. Plant in full sun to light shade in compost-enriched,
well-drained soil. These LOBELIAS need abundant moisture
during the growing season. Hardy to about 10°. [8, 9]

Loropetalum chinense. FRINGE FLOWER.
   3–6 ft. (China)

Small to medium-sized shrubs with oval leaves displayed in
flat sprays on arching branches. Lacy petaled flowers form
at the ends of the branches. They bloom mainly in late winter and spring but also sporadically throughout the year.
Loropetalum need good, compost-enriched soil that drains
well. Plant in full sun on the coast to light shade inland.
Hardy to about 5–10°.

◑ 'PLUM DELIGHT'. Stunning selection with deep purple
leaves and deep pink flowers. [3, 6]

◑ 'RAZZLEBERRI'. Leaves brownish purple; reddish violet
flowers. [3, 8]

Ⓐ *Lychnis coronaria.* ROSE CAMPION.

12 in. with 3 ft. flowering stalks (Southeastern Europe)
ROSE CAMPION is a reliable perennial that forms clumps
of woolly gray foliage. Brilliant magenta flowers in late
spring and summer rise on tall stems and last for some time.
Can self-sow in the garden. Plant in full sun in most soils
and give moderate water. Hardy to about 0°. [7]

Lysimachia. LOOSESTRIFE.

2–3 ft. (North America and Eurasia)
Vigorous, matting perennials that spread by underground
stems. Semideciduous in coastal areas to fully deciduous in
colder regions. Plant in full sun in most soils and give average water. Hardy to about 0°.

Ⓑ *CILIATA* 'PURPUREA'. Flowers to 2–3 ft. Reddish purple
leaves; small bright yellow flowers on tall stems appear in
summer. [6]

Ⓒ *NUMMULARIA* 'AUREA'. GOLDEN MONEYWORT. 2 in.
× spreading. Creeping perennial with golden foliage; looks
a little ragged in winter but brilliant the rest of year; color is
best in partial shade. [1, 4]

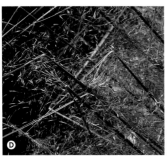

Ⓓ *Muhlenbergia filipes.* PURPLE MUHLY.

2½–3 ft. (Southeastern United States)
A winter-dormant species that carries wonderful, soft purple
flower bracts in the fall. Dormancy brings tan leaves and
dry seed heads that are very attractive in their own right.
When you see a mass of the airy purple flowers, you know
you have to grow this plant. When new growth appears
in spring I carefully cut back the older dry stems. Plant in
full sun in most soils and give average water. Hardy to
about 10°. [9]

❸ *Muhlenbergia rigens.* DEERGRASS.

3 ft. with flower stalks to 6 ft. (California to Texas, northern Mexico)

This perennial California native bunchgrass forms a dense, 6 ft.-wide clump of narrow green leaves that, with the flower stalks, create a fountainlike effect. Flowering peaks in late summer, but the stems persist for some time. The erect stems then tend to lean to the side, creating a slightly disheveled look. Best in full sun or light shade; tolerates most soils and needs regular watering. DEERGRASS is native to stream areas and likes consistent moisture; it looks poor when grown drier. (Note: I have moved this plant twice—once in summer and once in winter—and both times the move severely set the deergrass back. Perhaps it does not like to be moved.) Hardy to about 10°. [LINES THE OUT-SIDE OF THE STREAM GARDEN]

❸ *Myrsine africana.* AFRICAN BOXWOOD.

3–8 ft. (Azores, eastern and southern Africa, Afghanistan to Nepal)

Clipped BOXWOOD makes a tough, attractive, evergreen hedge. Small, dark green, shiny leaves add a formal touch to the garden. These plants are relatively pest-free and do well in a variety of soils, light or heavy, as long as runoff is good. Dark reddish stems are a little floppy in youth but stiffen with age and frequent pruning. Plant in full sun or light shade and supply moderate watering. Hardy to about 15°. [THROUGHOUT THE BOWL GARDEN]

A *Nandina domestica.* HEAVENLY BAMBOO.
2–6 ft. (India to Eastern Asia)

Evergreen shrubs with finely divided leaves on canelike stems. Plant in full sun to light shade. The unique coloring of Nandina will show better in the sun. Tough plants that tolerate most any soil or watering regime but are happiest with good soil and average water. Hardy to about 15°. [6]

B 'GULFSTREAM'. One of the best compact-growing varieties from a nursery in Monrovia; wonderful red color in winter. [3]

C 'LONGDEN PEARL'. Slow-growing, with striking white berries; does not color up in winter. [6]

D 'MOYER'S RED'. Upright growth with narrow leaves having a purplish cast; can turn brilliant red in winter. [6]

E 'WOOD'S DWARF'. 2 ft. Broad leaves forming a densely packed mound with bright red coloring in winter and a brilliant chartreuse in spring; a good accent plant. [9]

F *Nectaroscordum siculum.*
SICILIAN HONEY GARLIC.
To 2 ft. (France, Italy)

This is a woodland bulb that begins growth in winter and then flowers in early spring. The blossoms are pendulous and bell-shaped and colored creamy white, with pink tones and green at the base. Deciduous in summer, this bulb reliably comes back each year. Plant in full sun to light shade in well-drained soil and supply regular moisture during the growing season. Hardy to about −5°. [7]

G *Nemesia* 'Innocence'. NEMESIA.
12–15 in. (South Africa)

Nemesia are small, shrubby, evergreen perennials that seen to bloom almost year round. This variety has fragrant white flowers. It's best to shear off old blooms occasionally to refresh the plant. Plant in full sun to light shade in well-drained soil and supply average water. They may be short-lived but will often self-sow in surrounding areas. Hardy to about 25–27°. [1, 7]

H *Nepeta × faassenii* 'Blue Wonder'. CATMINT.
To 2 ft. (Garden origin)

Tough, rhizomatous perennial with aromatic, narrow, gray-green leaves that carry masses of small blue flower stalks from late spring through fall. Shear back faded blooms for repeat performance. If plants begin to look ratty, cut back to crown for fresh new growth. Plant in full sun in well-drained soil and supply moderate water. Hardy to about 0°. [8, 9]

I *Nicotiana* 'Lime Green'.
FLOWERING TOBACCO.
1½ ft. (Southern Brazil, northern Argentina)

FLOWERING TOBACCO is a tender perennial in our climate that gives us nearly nonstop blossoms. Not only can it seed itself but it can also resprout from the roots. There are many colors available, but 'Lime Green' is a special treat in the bright area of the garden. Typically, the large oval leaves and stems are sticky to the touch. Plant in full sun in a well-drained soil and give moderate watering. Hardy to at least 27°. [4, 9]

G

H

I

A *Nigella damascena.* LOVE-IN-A-MIST.
1–2½ ft. (North Africa, southern Europe)
Soft-textured, lacy leaves, lacinated flower petals, and inflated, papery seed pods attract us to growing this easy annual. Known mainly to be spring-flowering; later sowing in summer can even produce an early fall bloom. Flower colors range form white to blue to rose. Self-sows in the garden, giving the gardener free seedlings. Plant in full sun in most soils and supply average watering. [8]

B *Oenanthe japonica* 'Flamingo'.
FLOWERING CELERY.
To 1 ft. × spreading (India, Japan, Malaysia)
Lovely white variegated ground cover for shady areas. The leaves are narrowly toothed and colored a medium green, heavily splashed with white and tinted pink. Thrives in a moist spot in the garden and can actually grow in water. This is a very aggressive grower, so watch where you put it. Plants tend to mound up with time and can be sheared to the ground for fresh new growth. Plant in full sun on the coast to light shade elsewhere in most soils and give regular water. Deciduous with frost. Hardy to about 25°.
[1, 2, 7]

C *Ophiopogon planiscapus* 'Nigrescens'.
BLACK MONDO GRASS.
8 in. (Eastern Asia)
Evergreen perennial with narrow black leaves (new growth green) that form slow-growing clumps to 1 ft. across. MONDO GRASS spreads by underground rhizomes (albeit very slowly). Short stems with clusters of white flowers appear in late spring and early summer. Best planted in partial shade in well-drained soil and given regular water. Hardy to about 15°. [1, 2]

Origanum. ORNAMENTAL OREGANO.
(Mediterranean and southwestern Asia)
Many of the ORNAMENTAL OREGANOS make excellent
ground covers. Best planted in a well-drained soil in full
sun to light shade and given moderate water. Hardy to
about 18°.

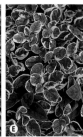

D 'BETTY ROLLINS'. Tight green foliage; excellent low
ground cover; 3–4 in. flower stalks of pink flowers in
summer. [4, 8]

E × *MAJORICUM* 'WELL SWEEP'. Low-growing mounds with
green leaves heavily splashed with white. [5, 7]

F *VULGARE* 'JIM BEST'. Ground cover with large roundish
leaves colored medium yellow and green. Although shy to
flower it can send up 1 ft. stems topped with light pink blossoms in summer. [5, 9]

G *Osmanthus heterophyllus* 'Goshiki'.
FALSE HOLLY.
    3–4 ft. (Japan, Taiwan)
FALSE HOLLY is a very versatile and fun plant to grow. It
will take sun or shade as well as a variety of soils and watering regimes and still look good. The leaves of 'Goshiki' are
a pink-orange maturing to yellow on a dark green. The leaf
edge is spined like a holly. They are slow-growing and nearly disease-free. Hardy to at least 15°. [3]

H *Oxalis* 'Garnet'. OXALIS.
    3–4 in. (South Africa)
Beautiful purple foliage and deep purple flowers during
winter and spring make this summer-deciduous bulb a
must for the garden. Relatively refined for Oxalis, it spreads
slowly. Can take year-round irrigation but will go dormant
in summer. Plant in full sun in well-drained soil and give
moderate water. Hardy to at least 27°. [2, 7, 8]

A *Papaver commutatum*. LADYBIRD POPPY.
12–15 in. (Caucasus, Asia Minor)
Here is an annual poppy that is a real standout. Hundreds of bright red flowers with black spots in the middle entertain everyone. Plant seeds in late fall or winter for spring bloom. Sow seeds on the surface with a light covering of sand. Can self-sow sparingly in the garden. Plant in full sun in well-drained soil and give average water. [9]

B *Papaver rhoeas*. RED FLANDERS POPPY.
3 ft. (Eurasia)
The name itself attracts our attention. Large, 3–4 in., bright red flowers from the fields of Flanders add a special spring touch to the garden. Plant seeds in late winter through spring and in early summer for successive crops. Sow seeds on the surface with a light covering of sand. Self-sows in the garden. Plant in full sun in well-drained soil and give average water. Annual. [6, 8, 9]

Papaver somniferum. BREADSEED POPPY.
3–4 ft. (Southeastern Europe and western Asia)
It just isn't a good spring without POPPIES in the garden. These tall annuals carry their flowers on terminal shoots. The peony form is very unusual, and many do not recognize them as POPPIES. Leaves are large and gray-green, with wavy edges, and are susceptible to powdery mildew. Spray with refined horticultural oil early and frequently for control. Sow seeds late fall through winter for spring bloom. Plant in full sun in well-drained soil and give average water.

C 'BLACK PEONY'. Hundreds of ruffled petals forming large, 3–4 in. balls. [8]
D 'LAVENDER BREADSEED'. Large, single-petaled lavender with reddish purple blotches. [7, 8, 9]
E 'WHITE PEONY'. Hundreds of ruffled petals forming large, 3–4 in. balls. [7, 9]

⊖ *Parahebe linifolia.*
10–12 in. (New Zealand)
A delightful subshrub with small, glossy, dark green leaves
and a generous supply of small white flowers that are present nearly all the time. Plant in full sun or light shade in
well-drained soil and give moderate water. Hardy to 15°
or less. [2, 3]

Pelargonium. GERANIUM.
The naming here is confusing to most people; the plants
they usually call GERANIUM are actually Pelargonium. True
GERANIUMS are generally low-growing, with narrow, trailing stems (though the popular 'Martha Washington' and
scented GERANIUMS have thick stems and are generally
bushlike in growth). Most Pelargonium are of easy growth
and are very tough plants. The zonal GERANIUMS—
Pelargonium × hortorum—require lots of feeding for good
growth. Budworms and rust plague them. Use them as
annuals, because they are spectacular when young and
fresh. Plant in full sun in most soils and give only moderate
water. Hardy to at least 25°.

⊙ *GRAVEOLENS* **'LADY PLYMOUTH'.** ROSE-SCENTED
LEAVED GERANIUM. 2–3 ft. Deeply cut medium green
leaves heavily splashed with creamy white, rose-scented
leaves, with light pink flowers in spring. It is always nice
to plant the scented-leaf varieties near a path where the
fragrance will be picked up when passing. [4]

⊕ × *HORTORUM* **'CRYSTAL PALACE GEM'.** 15 in. (Garden
origin). Bright yellow leaves with soft green centers; deep
pink flowers. [9]

⊙ × *HORTORUM* **'VANCOUVER CENTENNIAL'.** 12 in. (Garden
origin). Bronzy red-and-yellow leaves with reddish flowers.
[4, 9]

⊙ **'IRVINE'.** To 2 ft. (Garden origin). Brightly colored landscape perennial with reddish green leaves; covered with
pink-orange flowers from spring through summer and
sporadically during the rest of the year. [8]

⊗ *SIDOIDES.* 12 in. (South Africa). One-inch, rounded,
gray-green leaves support airy sprays of deep burgundy
flowers. Blooms for months on end from late winter into
summer, slowing down in late summer or early fall. [3, 7]

Penstemon. BEARD TONGUE.

To 2 ft. (North America)

Evergreen perennial shrublets with a long blooming period, from spring through fall, which grow from 1½ ft. to 3 ft. with narrow stems lined with lance-shaped leaves. Penstemon are best replaced every 3–4 years because they become somewhat woody. They are easy to propagate from cuttings and often root where a branch touches the ground. Cut back old flowering stems to 6 in. for stockier plants. Plant in full sun in a well-drained soil and supply moderate watering. Hardy to about 0°.

A 'BURGUNDY GLOW': Rich burgundy with pink throat; upright growth. [8, 9]
B 'LADY ALICE HINDLEY': Light blue with purple accent. [8]
C 'RASPBERRY FLAIR': Very large blossoms, raspberry-colored with white lines. [9]

D *Persicaria microcephala* 'Red Dragon'.
RED DRAGON KNOTWEED.

To 3 ft. (Garden origin)

Partially deciduous perennial with new leaves colored chocolate brown with darker triangle centers. Small sprays of white flowers in summer. Cut back in late winter for fresh new spring growth. A very refined, nonrunning selection that does not spread wildly in the garden. Plant in full sun to light shade in well-drained soil and give regular water. Hardy to about −15°. [2]

E *Persicaria virginiana.* KNOTWEED.

1½ –2 ft. (Himalayas, Japan, eastern North America)

Now here is an incredible foliage plant: green leaves with red chevrons and airy, sparkling red flower stalks. Flowering peaks during summer. Best used in light shade because the sun tends to burn the leaves a little. Self-sows religiously and completely deciduous in winter. Plant in light shade in well-drained soil and give regular water. Hardy to about −15°. [2]

Phormium. NEW ZEALAND FLAX.

(New Zealand)

Excellent, slow-growing accent plants with sword-shaped leaves. Phormium are very tough plants that require full sun or light shade, moderate water, and a fairly well-drained soil. Some cultivars can revert to green growth. Cut the green growth out, as it will overtake the rest of the plant. Hardy to about 15°.

F 'AMAZING RED'. To 3–4 ft. Deep reddish brown. [2]

G 'APRICOT QUEEN'. To 3 ft. Yellow with wide green margins and stripes; a fine center line and fine edge of deep red-brown. [4]

H 'CAROUSEL'. 4 ft. Bronze-green leaves with wide, creamy yellow and pink edges; close to 'Maori Queen'. [9]

I *COOKIANUM* 'MAORI QUEEN'. To 3 ft. Bronze-green leaves with wide pink stripes, medium yellow and bronze outer edges. [4]

J *COOKIANUM* SUBSP. *HOOKERI* 'TRICOLOR'. 2½–3 ft. Leaves striped green and cream. [4]

K 'GUARDSMAN'. 5–6 ft. Bronzy maroon leaves with deep red stripes. [4]

L 'JACK SPRATT'. 2 ft. Dark chocolate leaves. [4; ALSO SURROUNDS BOWL GARDEN]

M 'SURFER'. To 2½ ft. Bronze leaves with a reddish edge. [4; ALSO SURROUNDS BOWL GARDEN]

N *TENAX* 'BRONZE BABY'. Chocolate brown leaves to 2½ ft. [3]

O *TENAX* 'YELLOW WAVE'. To 3 ft. Leaves yellow with thin green stripes; more yellow than 'Apricot Queen'. [4]

P 'TINY TIM'. 2½ ft. Green leaves with a reddish bronze edge. [SURROUNDS BOWL GARDEN]

Ⓐ *Phygelius* × *rectus*. CAPE FUCHSIA.
3 ft. (South Africa)

CAPE FUCHSIA is a woody stemmed perennial with droop-ing FUCHSIA-like flowers. They are easy to culture and spread by underground stems. Once a year I prune back the spreading clumps, removing some of the rooted stems. Plant in full sun or light shade in most soils and give moder-ate water. Hardy to at least 15°.

'SENSATION'. Reddish violet flowers. [8]

Ⓑ *Platanus* × *acerifolia* 'Yarwood'.
YARWOOD LONDON PLANE TREE.
30–40 ft. × 40–80 ft. (Garden origin)

The London plane tree is a close relative of our native sycamore. London plane trees are large, fast-growing, deciduous trees. The leaves of the variety YARWOOD are exceptionally large, reaching 8–10 inches across. YARWOOD is also the most disease-resistant of the lot, with the foliage rarely suffering from anthracnose, which ruins most other varieties. The bark is smooth and cream colored. Tolerant of most soils; plant in full sun and give this tree space to grow. Hardy to about –15°. [LINES THE STREAM GARDEN]

Ⓒ *Platycodon grandiflorus* subsp. *mariesii*.
BALLOON FLOWER.
To 1–1½ ft. (China, Japan)

This Campanula relative has large, open, starlike flowers in summer. The name comes from the balloonlike buds that form on thin but stiff stems. Dying back completely in win-ter, BALLOON FLOWER sprouts from large, fleshy rhi-zomes in spring. Avoid disturbing the roots; they can take a season or two to settle in well. This selection carries blue flowers, which seem to be the most vigorous, but there are white and pink forms also. Plant in full sun in most soils and give regular water. Hardy to about 0°. [8]

◑ *Plectranthus forsteri* 'Gigantea Aurea.'
SPUR FLOWERS.

To 3 ft. (Eastern Australia, Fiji, New Caledonia)
This is a great foliage plant with large, soft, felty leaves
variegated green and yellow. Plectranthus are perennial
members of the mint family, which prosper in shady areas.
This selection has never flowered for me but should have
white flowers. Best planted in light shade in a well-drained
soil and given moderate watering. Hardy to at least 28°
and will resprout after harder frosts. [1]

ⓔ *Portulacaria afra* 'Variegata.'
VARIEGATED ELEPHANT BUSH.

6–10 ft. (South Africa)
ELEPHANT BUSH is a succulent shrub or small tree that
forms a very thick trunk resembling an elephant's foot. This
selection has small leaves edged in creamy yellow-white.
Although very drought-tolerant, ELEPHANT BUSH will also
do well with regular water. A great accent with ECHEVE-
RIAS at the base. Plant in full sun to light shade in well-
drained soil and give only moderate water. Hardy to at
least 27°. [1, 7]

ⓕ *Punica granatum* var. *nana*.
DWARF POMEGRANATE.

3–4 ft. (Southeastern Europe to Himalayas)
DWARF POMEGRANATE is a slow-growing shrub with
beautiful, glossy, golden green foliage that can be semideciduous even in warmer areas. Ornamental red fruits
follow orange-red flowers, which begin in spring and
persist during fall. Plant in full sun (best color in full sun).
Is tolerant of most soils; thrives in high heat. Give
moderate water. Hardy to about 15°. [9]

A *Ranunculus ficaria* 'Brazen Hussy.'
LESSER CELANDINE.
  2 in. with flowers to 6 in. (Northern Europe)
The name 'Brazen Hussy' hits the mark for this tuberous
rooted perennial. The low-growing leaves are deep bronze-
green, contrasting with flowers of brilliant yellow. Plants
begin growth in early winter and are completely dormant in
summer. LESSER CELANDINE can be invasive in some
conditions, notably in moister climates. Plant in full sun to
light shade in well-drained soil and give regular moisture
during the growing season. Hardy to about –15°. [2]

B *Rhodanthemum hosmariense.*
  8 in. with flowers to 12 in. (Morocco)
The finely cut silvery foliage that forms tight mounds and
the clear white 2 in. flowers make this a good choice for the
front of the border. Good drainage is essential, along with
full sun and moderate watering. Blooms profusely late winter and spring and sporadically throughout the year. Hardy
to about 25°. [7]

Rhododendron. AZALEA.
Robert Irwin's sculptural azalea pool is one of the focal
points in the garden. AZALEAS can be challenging plants
in Southern California due to our alkaline soils, salty water,
and hot, dry winds. To guard against alkalinity the plants
are set in a special blend of pure peat moss. AZALEAS
are prone to fungal root diseases. To protect them, always
plant the crown of the plant a little higher than the surrounding ground. Although often thought of as shade
plants, there are many varieties that have been developed
for full-sun exposure. Regular watering with very good
drainage is important.

C 'APPLE BLOSSOM'. White, flushed and striped with
pink. [10]
D 'HINO CRIMSON'. Bronzy green foliage, red flowers. [10]
E 'SNOW'. Pure white. [10]

Rosa. ROSE.

Roses are the most gardenesque features of the plant world. Everyone grows some, but each area will find only a select few that perform well without persistent disease problems. The ones listed below have proven to be great plants for coastal Southern California (some are chosen for color rather then disease resistance). Roses should be planted in full sun, with good air circulation, in a compost-enriched, well-drained soil; they should be given regular water. Hardy to about 15°.

F **'DUBLIN BAY'.** Climber with deep red flowers and fairly disease-resistant foliage. [7]

G **'FLUTTERBYE'.** Climber with single flowers that change from yellow to peach. [9]

H **'GINGERSNAP'.** Vivid orange flowers, a fantastic color; mildew-prone. [9]

I **'ICEBERG'.** An almost perfect single white rose; good glossy foliage. [3]

J **'MEIDILAND RED'.** Single, bright red flowers with white centers. [6, 8]

K **'SEA FOAM'.** Double white blossoms with a pink tinge; mildew-resistant. [7, 8]

L **'SHOWBIZ'.** Rich deep red; some mildew. [9]

M **'SUN FLARE'.** Rich yellow. [9]

N **'SUNSPRITE'.** Bright yellow; some mildew. [9]

O **'TRUMPETER'.** 2½ ft. Shrub rose with nearly continuous red flowers; very clean, almost no disease. [3, 8, 9]

P *WICHURANA* **'VARIEGATA'.** VARIEGATED MEMORIAL ROSE. Climbing, mound-forming rose with small dark green leaves heavily marbled with white and pink; small clusters of white flowers. [7]

A *Rubus cockburnianus.* GHOST BRAMBLE.
To 4–8 ft. (China)

GHOST BRAMBLE is another winter-deciduous plant that
we use for its colorful bark, in this case white. White is a
great accent not only with gray but also with the brighter
yellows and reds. (Adding a touch of white into a bright
combination is a wonderful Irwin touch.) This BRAMBLE is
not very exciting when in leaf, and it can spread to form a
thicket, so I remove it in spring to summer over back at my
nursery, returning it to the garden in late fall. Hardy to
about –15° [1, 2, 9]

B *Rudbeckia hirta.* BLACK-EYED SUSAN
(or CONEFLOWER)
    2–3 ft. (Central United States)

Showy perennials having lance-shaped green leaves and
bright yellow flowers with dark centers throughout summer
and fall. Plants will be semideciduous to fully deciduous in
winter, and crowns can occasionally rot during a wet winter.
Deadhead old flowers for longer bloom period. Plant in full
sun in fairly well-drained soil and give moderate water.
Hardy to about 0° [9]

C *Rumex sanguineus.* BLOODY DOCK.
    12–15 in. (Europe, North Africa, southwestern Asia)

A valuable foliage plant that is a relative of rhubarb, this
perennial has deep green leaves ribbed with red veins.
Although our plants have never flowered, the blossoms
should be green with reddish tinges. Plant in light shade
in compost-enriched, well-drained soil and give regular
watering. Plants can self-sow in the garden or increase
by division. Hardy to about –5° [3]

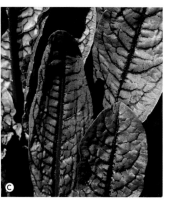

❶ *Russelia equisetiformis.* CORAL FOUNTAIN.
3–4 ft. (Mexico)

Russelia sends out long, arching, green stems, creating an
excellent accent in the garden. Bright red flowers spring
and summer add splashes of color to the nearly leafless
stems. In warm coastal areas CORAL FOUNTAIN can be
nearly ever-blooming. Best planted in light shade in a well-
drained soil with regular watering. Hardy to about 28–32°.
[3, 4]

❷ 'AUREA'. With lemon-yellow flowers. [2, 3]

❸ *Ruta graveolens* 'Variegata'. VARIEGATED RUE.
2 ft. (Southeastern Europe)

This perennial herb is sought after for the garden because
of its lovely blue-green foliage. The new growth is splashed
with creamy yellow. Small, fernlike leaflets form billowy
mounds. Stalks of small yellow flowers add contrast to the
foliage in spring and early summer. Plant in full sun in a
well-drained soil and give moderate water. Hardy to at least
28°. [7]

Salix. WILLOW.
(Worldwide except Australia)

WILLOWS combine a very large group of plants, mainly
from the cooler regions of the Northern Hemisphere, but
there are a few in the Southern Hemisphere as well. Most
enjoy a moist location, such as near streams, but again
there are a few odd dry members. We grow these plants
for their dormant winter look. As with the SHRUBBY DOG-
WOODS they often have colorful and interesting bark.
It is this bare look that helps to reinforce winter's feel here
in evergreen Southern California. I push the envelope by
pulling the leaves off in late fall to force dormancy and
color up the stems. We lift the WILLOWS and put them
in pots to summer over at my nursery, returning them in
the fall to the garden.

❹ 'FLAME'. FLAME WILLOW. Brilliant orange stems on
new growth. [4, 9]

❺ *IRRORATA.* BLUE-STEM WILLOW. Pale blue-gray bark.
[3, 7, 8]

❻ *PURPUREA* 'PENDULA'. BLUE FOUNTAIN WILLOW. Like
the BLUE-STEM WILLOW, but with pendulous stems. [8]

Salvia. SAGE.
(Worldwide)

SAGES are a very diverse group of mint family relatives. Plant in full sun in a well-drained soil and supply moderate water.

Ⓐ *BLEPHAROPHYLLA.* EYELASH-LEAVED SAGE (Mexico). 2 ft. Small-scale Salvia with rich green leaves tinged with purple and having bright orange-red flowers spring and summer and sporadically year-round. Spreads by underground stolons. Hardy to about 20°. [9]

Ⓑ *BUCHANANII.* BUCHANAN'S FUCHSIA SAGE. 2 ft. Deep green glossy leaves on stems that spread by underground stolons. It produces stunning, deep fuchsia-pink flowers late spring to summer and sporadically into fall. Hardy to about 22°. [8]

Ⓒ *CHAMAEDRYOIDES.* GERMANDER SAGE. 2–3 ft. One of the best compact Salvia with small gray-green leaves and with nearly everblooming, bright blue flowers in coastal areas. Very good for tough dry areas but also tolerates more irrigation. Shear off old flowers occasionally for a clean, compact bush. Hardy to about 15–20°. [7]

Ⓓ *DORISIANA.* FRUIT-SCENTED SAGE. 4–6 ft. Lime-green leaves have a fruity scent, with remarkable, rich pink flowers in late winter and spring. Cut back regularly for compact growth. Hardy to about 20°. [9]

Ⓔ × *SYLVESTRIS* **'MAY NIGHT'.** 2 ft. Upright stalks of purple flowers can occur nearly year-round if old flowers are removed from this bushy perennial. Main bloom period is early spring through summer, with occasional blooms into fall. Hardy to about 0°. [8, 9]

Ⓕ *VERTICILLATA* **'PURPLE RAIN'.** 1½ ft. Semideciduous even in coastal areas, 'Purple Rain' has wide, felty, gray-green leaves that support purple flower stalks from spring to summer. Mildew can sometimes be a problem; the best solution is to cut away infected leaves to allow for new growth. Hardy to about –5°. [8]

ⓖ *Santolina chamaecyparissus* 'Lemon Queen.'
LAVENDER COTTON.

2 ft. (Mediterranean)

'Lemon Queen' is a compact shrub with finely dissected, silvery gray-green leaves and rounded clusters of flowers in summer. Most of the Santolina have bright yellow flowers, but this selection is favored with soft, lemon-yellow blossoms. To prosper, these Mediterranean plants require full sun and good drainage and moderate watering. Hardy to about 0°. [7]

Sedum. STONECROP.

2–3 in. (Mountains in Northern Hemisphere)

Succulent perennials that need very good drainage to prosper. Moderate watering with full sun on the coast to light shade inland. Hardy to about 10°.

ⓗ *CONFUSUM.* Yellow-green foliage; yellow flowers begin late winter and last into spring. [1, 4]

ⓘ 'FLORI'. Carpeting, deep green foliage with reddish tints in winter; yellow flowers show sporadically throughout the year. [2, 5]

ⓙ *FORSTERIANUM* 'BLUE CARPET'. Carpeting, blue-green, short-needle foliage and yellow flowers late winter to early summer. [1]

ⓚ *MAKINA* 'OGON'. Carpeting, bright yellow leaves and yellow flowers. Best in light shade. [9]

ⓛ *Sempervivum arachnoideum.*
COBWEB HOUSELEEK.

3–4 in. (Mountains in Europe and Asia)

HOUSELEEKS are evergreen perennials that form dense clusters of tight rosettes. COBWEB HOUSELEEK is a quick grower, with small rosettes of gray-green leaves that are covered with white hairs, ¾ in. rosy pink flowers on 6–8 in. stems in summer. Good drainage is essential, with moderate watering and full sun on the coast to light shade inland. A perfect plant for crevices in walls. Watch for rots in summer. Hardy to about 0°. [1]

A *Senecio confusus.* MEXICAN FLAME VINE.

Vine (Mexico to Honduras)

This striking vine has glossy green leaves that carry brilliant orange DAISY-like flowers throughout the warm months of the year. Deciduous in colder climates but can behave as an evergreen in milder coastal areas. A good orange is hard to find, and often hard to use, but this is a must for the bright areas of the garden. Plant in full sun in compost-enriched soil and supply average water. Hardy to about 20°. [9]

B *Silene uniflora* 'Druett's Variety.' VARIEGATED SEA-CAMPION.

6 in. (Western Europe)

Excellent ground-cover perennial with light blue-green leaves strongly splashed with white and having white flowers. VARIEGATED SEA-CAMPION makes a good show spilling over rocks and walls. Plant in full sun in well-drained soil and give moderate watering for good growth. Hardy to about 10°. [4, 7]

C *Solanum jasminoides* 'Album.' POTATO VINE.

Vine (Brazil)

Pure white flowers year-round in coastal areas make this a perfect choice for any garden. Easy and fast growing, with narrow, rich green leaves that can have a purple tinge. Plant in full sun in most soils and supply moderate water. Hardy to about 15°. [7, 8]

◉ *Solanum pyracanthum.*

To 5 ft. (Madagascar)

A very unusual member of the genus with stems that are clothed with orange thorns and carry light lavender flowers from early spring through late fall. It seems everyone is attracted to this plant and always comments on it. Can reseed in the garden. Plant in full sun to light shade in a well-drained soil and supply moderate water. Hardy to at least 28°. [2, 9]

Solenostemon scutellarioides. COLEUS.

1 ft. (Southeast Asia)

Here is a common plant given a new and strange name. We all know them as COLEUS and there are countless exciting cultivars. They make good houseplants but can be grown outside in mild winter areas year-round. It's always best to remove the stalks of the blue flower because this keeps the plant in vegetative growth. Best in partial shade in compost-enriched, well-drained soil and with regular water. Not hardy.

❸ 'DUCK'S FOOT'. 1 ft. Small, red-velvet leaves edged with yellow-green; deeply lobed. [9]

❺ 'PINEAPPLE'. 15 in. Deep red with wide, yellow-green, serrated edges; turns all red in more sun. [4]

❻ 'ULRICK'. 15 in. Deep red with considerable yellow and green mottling; leaf edge rounded. [2]

❹ *Sparaxis tricolor.* HARLEQUIN FLOWER.

6–15 in. (South Africa)

HARLEQUIN FLOWERS are bright orange with yellow centers and black lines in the throat; there are hybrids in many colors, white to red to pink. They are winter- and spring-growing corms that are dormant during summer. They are easy to cultivate and can take year-round irrigation. Plant 3–4 in. deep in full sun in very well-drained soil and give average water. Hardy to about 20°. [9]

A *Spiraea japonica* 'Gold Flame.'
GOLDEN-LEAVED JAPANESE SPIRAEA.
2–3 ft. (China, Japan)
'Gold Flame' has a long deciduous period but is worth the wait when spring brings amazing golden foliage that has a reddish pink hue. Clusters of rose-pink flowers complement the colorful leaves. Plant in full sun to light shade in well-drained soil and give moderate water. Hardy to less than 0°. [4]

Stachys byzantina. LAMBS' EARS.
5–10 in. (Caucasus to Iran)
LAMBS' EARS is a tough ground cover with large, felty, gray leaves. 1–2 ft. stems of lavender flowers appear in summer. May look ragged after flowering, so cut to ground and allow new foliage to grow back. Hardy to about 0°.

B 'HELEN VON STEIN'. Robust form with larger leaves. [1, 2]
C 'SILVER CARPET'. Does not produce flowers. [1, 2]

D *Stigmaphyllon ciliatum.* ORCHID VINE.
Woody vine (Belize to Uruguay)
Evergreen in milder climates, ORCHID VINE is fast growing, with twining stems clothed in paired leaflets. Bright yellow flowers resembling Oncidium orchids decorate the plant in summer and early fall, but some sporadic flowering can occur year-round in milder areas. Give this vine full sun or light shade with compost-enriched soil and supply average watering for successful growth. Hardy to about 25°. [9]

❸ *Stipa ramosissima*. PILLAR OF SMOKE.

3–6 ft. (Eastern Australia)

PILLAR OF SMOKE is an evergreen, clump-forming perennial grass. Thin, bamboo-like canes are topped with large flower panicles, 6–10 in. long. New panicles emerge in summer and look good for many months. Even the older flowers are attractive, giving this plant year-round interest. Plant in full sun in a well-drained soil and supply moderate water. Hardy to about 18°. [IN POTS ON THE PLAZA]

❺ *Strobilanthes isophyllus*. BEDDING CONEHEAD.

2 ft. (Northeast India)

A lovely, small-scale perennial with very deep green leaves that turn purple-green and carry airy, very pale blue flowers in late winter to early spring and sporadically throughout the year. After flowering, plants look a bit ratty and should be lightly pruned. Best in light shade but will tolerate full sun on the coast, where the color deepens considerably. Can self-sow in the garden. Plant in compost-enriched, well-drained soil and give moderate water. Hardy to at least 28°. [7, 8]

❻ *Tagetes* 'Granada'. DWARF SINGLE FRENCH MARIGOLD.

8–12 in.

I find the double floral heads of most MARIGOLDS to be just a little too large and the colors too simple. 'Granada' is a small plant with small single heads colored deep orange-red and yellow. It's a very happy combination and fills up all those front-of-the-border areas in summer. Sow seed in spring for early summer blooms. Sowing late in summer will give additional color through late fall. Plant in full sun in most soils and give average water. Annual. [9]

❶ *Tanacetum parthenium* 'Aureum'.
GOLDEN FEVERFEW.

2–2½ ft. (Europe, Caucasus)

An old-fashioned perennial with amazing chartreuse-colored foliage and white daisy flowers that are present nearly year-round with a peak in May to August. Plant in full sun to light shade in most soils with moderate watering. GOLDEN FEVERFEW will self-sow in the garden and spread its chartreuse coloring into unexpected areas. Hardy to about 25°. [4, 9]

❷ *Tanacetum ptarmiciflorum*. SILVER LACE.

3–4 ft. (Grand Canary Island)

Fabulous silvery gray, fernlike foliage makes this a special treat in the garden. Flower buds form in late winter, leading to a brilliant display of blossoms from spring to early summer. Sprays of small white flowers are the perfect accent to the silver foliage. In its second year the foliage will be left atop bare stems. Prune back to 6–8 in., a few stems at a time, to rejuvenate a compact specimen. Plant in full sun in well-drained soil and supply moderate watering. Hardy to about 25°. [7]

Thalictrum. MEADOW RUE.

(North temperate regions)

Perennials with dissected blue-green leaves that carry tall airy flower stalks. Light shade, compost-enriched soil, and regular watering are needed for good growth. Hardy to about 0°.

❸ *DELAVAYI* 'HEWITT'S DOUBLE'. 12 in. Tall airy flower stalks with ½ in. pale lavender blossoms in summer; can be short-lived in warmer areas. [2]

❹ *FLAVUM* SUBSP. *GLAUCUM*. 12–15 in. Blue-gray foliage resembles that of COLUMBINES; tall flower stalks (to 4 ft.) appear in late spring and early summer and are topped with 1 in. balls of soft yellow blossoms. Tolerates more sun in coastal areas and can be evergreen there. [9]

Thymus. THYME.
   2 in. to 1 ft. (Eurasia)

THYMES are perennial subshrubs with highly aromatic leaves. The flat-growing varieties make excellent ground covers when given a well-drained site in the garden. I like to plant them near the tops of slopes, where they appreciate the drainage and receive less but still regular water. Root rots can present a problem during the warm summer months. Consider appropriate fungicides for favorite plants. Blooming times are late spring to early summer for most varieties. Plant in full sun to light shade in a very well-drained soil and supply average water. Hardy to at least 0°.

E × *CITRIODORUS* 'LIME'. Lime-green foliage on mounding plants; wonderfully scented leaves; pink flowers. [4]

F *SERPHYLLUM* 'ELFIN'. MOTHER OF THYME. Very small, tight-growing leaves; good between stepping stones; one of the easiest to grow; pink flowers. [5]

G 'TRANSPARENT YELLOW'. Flat-growing selection with yellowish green leaves. [4]

Tibouchina. PRINCESS FLOWER
(or GLORY BUSH)
   (Brazil)

Prized plants with oval leaves colored light green and covered with velvety, soft hairs. The curiously ribbed leaves grace a somewhat open framework, and branches support rich purple flower clusters. Prune lightly to keep the bush more compact. Cooler winter temperatures bring a reddish tinge to the leaves. PRINCESS FLOWER will often get tip burn in Southern California and may be better planted in a more acid soil. Plant in full sun to light shade in compost-enriched soil and supply average water. Hardy to about 25–28°.

H *HETEROMALLA.* 5–6 ft. Clusters of smaller, 1 in. flowers with larger, 4–5 in. leaves; flowers in late fall and winter. [8, 9]

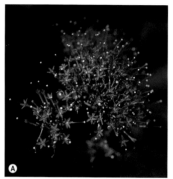

A *Trachelium caeruleum* 'Hamer Pandora'.
BLUE THROATWORT.

1½ ft. (Mediterranean)

This is an exciting selection of an old favorite perennial. 'Hamer Pandora' has purple-bronze leaves and deep purple flowers. The crown of the plant has narrowly pointed leaves and sends up erect stems topped with large heads of small flowers spring to summer. A good cut flower for the arranger. Grow in full sun in well-drained soil and supply moderate water. Hardy to about 20°. [8]

B *Trachelospermum jasminoides* 'Tricolor'.
TRICOLOR STAR JASMINE.

Vine to 20 ft. (China)

A superb form of the common STAR JASMINE, this variegated selection has new leaves molted with whitish yellow, pink, and bronze and carries highly fragrant flowers in late spring and early summer. Plant in full sun or light shade in most soils and supply average watering. Hardy to about 15°. [1, 2]

Trifolium. CLOVER.

2–4 in. (Garden origin)

Exciting selections of common CLOVER with highly ornamental leaves. Typical white flowers add to the charm of these interesting ground-cover perennials. Plant in full sun to light shade in most soils and supply moderate water. Can look a little ratty in the heat of summer but generally comes back well. Hardy to at least 25°.

C *PRATENSE* 'SUSAN SMITH'. GOLDEN CLOVER. Bright green leaves heavily veined with yellow; sends out long runners that should be tip-pruned for compactness; pink flowers early summer to fall. [2, 4]

D *REPENS* 'ATROPURPUREUM'. PURPLE-LEAVED CLOVER. Leaves heavily marked with purplish brown and edged in green; white flowers. [6, 8]

E *REPENS* 'GREEN ICE'. VARIEGATED CLOVER. Rich green leaves edged with mint green; white flowers early summer to fall. [2]

⦿ *Tropaeolum majus.* NASTURTIUM.
Annual vine (South America)

The common bright orange NASTURTIUM is one of
Robert Irwin's favorite plants. The full hue of its color,
the twining habit that mixes so well with other plants, and
the soft green foliage always bring a favorable comment
from him. Tropaeolum enjoy a well-drained soil with either
full sun or light shade. I like to soak the seeds in warm
water for 24 hours before sowing. They can be started
nearly anytime in our mild climate. Supply moderate
water and enjoy their ease of growth; they often reseed
year after year. Annual. [4]

⦿ *Tulbaghia violacea* 'Silver Lace.'
VARIEGATED SOCIETY GARLIC.
1½–2 ft. (South Africa)

SOCIETY GARLIC is one of those very utilitarian and near-
foolproof plants used in gardens. This selection has leaves
edged in creamy white. Plants give off a garlic-like smell,
especially after being pruned or bruised and on warmer
days. A very long blooming period begins in March and
April and extends into September and October. Plant in full
sun to light shade in most soils and give moderate water.
Hardy to 20–25°. [MIDDLE RING SURROUNDING THE BOWL
GARDEN]

Tulipa. TULIP.
10–24 in. (Europe, southern Eurasia)

TULIPS are a little out of place in our warm climate, but
with sufficient chilling in the crisper of your refrigerator
(6–8 weeks) they make a fine show in spring. They are
really only good for one season, with new bulbs purchased
each year.

⊞ 'NEGRITA'. Deep Concord-grape color with deep purple
veins. [6, 8]

⊙ 'SHIRLEY'. White-edged, lightly suffused with soft purple.
[6, 8]

❶ *Uncinia uncinata.* RED HOOK SEDGE.
12–15 in. (New Zealand)

A terrific accent plant, this evergreen perennial sedge has reddish bronze leaves. Best in partial shade with compost-enriched, moist soil. Leaf tips tend to look tattered, so shear lightly for new growth. Propagation is from seed because they resent division. The young plants are slow in growth but well worth the wait. Hardy to about 15°. [1, 2, 6]

❷ *Ursinia anethoides.* SUNSHINE DAISY.
8–12 in. (South Africa)

Beautiful, fernlike foliage, a light yellow-green in color, adorns this small perennial shrub that is normally grown as an annual. Bright orange daisy flowers on slender stems add excitement to any area. Can be grown from seed at any time of the year, but plants do best when planted out in the cooler months, gaining a larger size and flowering for a longer period. Plant in full sun in well-drained soil and give average water. Hardy to about 15°. [9]

❸ *Verbascum chaixii* 'Album'.
NETTLE-LEAVED MULLEIN.
Flowers 2–3 ft. (Europe)

NETTLE-LEAVED MULLEIN is a perennial that forms 1 ft. rosettes of low-growing basal leaves. Erect spikes of white flowers rise late winter to early summer. Plants can reseed in the garden. Plant in full sun to light shade in well-drained soil and supply moderate watering. Hardy to about 0°. [7]

❶ *Verbena bonariensis.*

3–6 ft. (South America)

Tall airy spikes topped with clusters of small lavender flowers make this a must for intermixing with other plants. The flowering period is very long, spring until fall. By itself it is a fine plant, but its appearance coming up through others— especially those with different leaf sizes and textures— makes this plant indispensable. Can be grown from seed at nearly any time of the year and planted out also at any time. Self-sows reliably in the garden. Powdery mildew can be a problem, so regular sprays of refined horticultural oil are recommended. Plant in full sun in most soils and give average water. Hardy to about 18°. [8, 9]

❷ *Verbena × hybrida* 'Tapien Blue'.
COMMON VERBENA.

Flat-spreading ground cover

There are many forms of Verbena that are used as quick fillers. This one is very flat-growing, having leaves rich green in color, and is very floriferous; the flower color is a rich blue-purple. VERBENA tends to burn out after one season and thus is best replanted each year. Powdery mildew can damage the foliage, but it is really not worth spraying. Plant in full sun to light shade in most soils and give average water. Hardy to about 25°. [3, 8]

❸ *Veronica peduncularis* 'Georgia Blue'.
SPEEDWELL.

2 in. (Turkey, Caucasus, Ukraine)

'Georgia Blue' is a mat-forming perennial with a very long blooming period, late winter to spring and sporadically throughout the year. Plant in full sun in a well-drained soil and give moderate watering. In hotter inland areas plant in light shade. Hardy to about 0°. [3]

Ⓐ *Viola tricolor* 'Prince Henry'.
JOHNNY-JUMP-UP.

4 in. (Europe, Asia)

'Prince Henry' is an all-purple-colored form of the old-fashioned JOHNNY-JUMP-UP. Considered an annual or short-lived perennial, JOHNNY-JUMP-UP will self-sow in the garden, coming up in surprising places. Late-winter- and spring-flowering. Robert Irwin and I found this in a garden in Oregon and were given seeds. Plant in full sun to light shade in most soils and give average water. [6, 8]

Ⓑ *Vitis vinifera* 'Purpurea'.
PURPLE-LEAVED GRAPE.

6–12 ft. (North temperate regions)

Foliage color plays an important role in the garden. Purple-leaved plants create magic in many settings. Use against yellows and chartreuse, which activate and brighten the combination; with greens and grays, they enhance and solidify the groupings. This compact selection of PURPLE-LEAVED GRAPE adds these qualities to the gray, subdued area of the Central Garden. The fruit is small and passable in taste, but the unique color helps build on the quiet strength found in this area. Mildew is a persistent problem; spray with refined horticultural oil. Plant in full sun in a well-drained soil and supply moderate water. Hardy to about 0°. [7]

Ⓒ *Watsonia intermedia.* PINK BUGLE LILY.

2 ft. (South Africa)

In the trade this bulb is sold as *Watsonia intermedia* (even though the species name, *intermedia*, is not valid). While not a true species, this bulb is a reliable performer. Its 2 ft. height makes it an ideal size for the garden. Spring brings pink, tubular flowers. Plant in full sun in well-drained soil and give moderate water. Hardy to 20–25°. [9]

PLANT LOCATION GUIDE, MAP, AND INDEX OF SCIENTIFIC AND COMMON NAMES

AREA 1

Abelia × *grandiflora* 'Confetti'
Agapanthus 'Stripes'
Arabis procurrens 'Variegata'
Athanasia acerosa
Calluna vulgaris
  'Peter Sparkes', 'Tib'
Carex testacea
Cerinthe major
Chondropetalum tectorum
Convolvulus cneorum
Crassula ovata 'Tricolor'
Echeveria 'Afterglow', 'Dondo',
  'Doris Taylor', 'Lola', 'Perle
  von Nurnberg'
Echeveria subsessilis
Erysimum 'Bowles' Mauve'
Eschscholzia californica
Euphorbia rigida
Euphorbia tirucallii 'Sticks of Fire'
Helichrysum 'Icicles'
Helleborus argutifolius
  'Janet Starnes'
Kalanchoe pumila
Kalanchoe thyrsiflora
Lavandula × *heterophylla*
  'Goodwin Creek'
Libertia peregrinans
Limonium psilocladium
Lobelia erinus 'Crystal Palace'
Lysimachia nummularia 'Aurea'
Nemesia 'Innocence'
Oenanthe japonica 'Flamingo'
Ophiopogon planiscapus
  'Nigrescens'
Plectranthus forsteri
  'Gigantica Aurea'
Portulacaria afra 'Variegata'
Rubus cockburnianus
Sedum confusum
Sedum forsterianum 'Blue Carpet'
Sempervivum arachnoideum
Stachys byzantina 'Helen von
  Stein', 'Silver Carpet'
Trachelospermum jasminoides
  'Tricolor'
Uncinia uncinata

AREA 2

Abutilon × *hybridum* 'Savitzii'
Adenanthos drummondii
Agapanthus 'Stripes'
Arctotis 'Torch Purple'
Astelia chathamica 'Silver Spear'
Astelia nivicola 'Red Gem'
Athanasia acerosa
Ballota nigra 'Archer's Variety'
Begonia 'Paul Hernandez'
Calandrinia grandiflora

Callicarpa bodinieri var. *giraldii*
  'Profusion'
Canna 'Stuttgart'
Carex hachijoensis 'Evergold'
Cerinthe major
Choisya ternata 'Sundance'
Convolvulus cneorum
Cornus stolonifera 'Flaverimea'
Deschampsia cespitosa
  'Northern Lights'
Dianella tasmanica 'Blushy'
Dudleya pulverulenta
Echeveria 'Lola'
Echeveria subsessilis
Erodium × *variabile* 'Album'
Eryngium 'Sapphire Blue'
Erysimum 'Bowles' Mauve'
Eschscholzia californica
Eschscholzia californica maritima
Euphorbia characias
  subsp. *wulfenii*
Fallopia japonica 'Variegata'
Farfugium japonicum
  'Argenteum', 'Crispatum'
Festuca 'Siskiyou Blue'
Fuchsia thymifolia 'Variegata'
Fuchsia triphylla 'Firecracker'
Gazania 'Trailing White'
Geranium 'Stanhoe'
Geranium harveyi
Glaucium flavum
Hebe pimeloides 'Quicksilver'
Helleborus argutifolius
  'Janet Starnes'
Helleborus foetidus
  'Chedglow', 'Red Silver'
Helleborus orientalis
  'Concord', 'Slate'
Hunnemannia fumariifolia
Isopogon formosus
Ixia viridiflora
Lavandula × *heterophylla*
  'Goodwin Creek'
Limonium psilocladium
Oenanthe japonica 'Flamingo'
Ophiopogon planiscapus
  'Nigrescens'
Oxalis 'Garnet'
Parahebe linifolia
Persicaria microcephala
  'Red Dragon'
Persicaria virginiana
Phormium 'Amazing Red'
Ranunculus ficaria
  'Brazen Beauty'
Rubus cockburnianus
Russelia equisetiformis
Russelia equisetiformis 'Aurea'
Sedum 'Flori'
Solanum pyracanthum

Solenostemon scutellarioides
  'Ulrick'
Stachys byzantina 'Helen von
  Stein', 'Silver Carpet'
Thalictrum delvayi
  'Hewitt's Double'
Trachelospermum jasminoides
  'Tricolor'
Trifolium pratense 'Susan Smith'
Trifolium repens 'Green Ice'
Uncinia uncinata

AREA 3

Acer palmatum var. *dissectum*
  'Ever Red'
Adenanthos drummondii
Alyogyne hakeifolia
Anemone × *hybrida*
  'Honorine Jobert'
Angelica pachycarpa
Anigozanthos flavidus
  'Bush Sunset'
Anthriscus sylvestris 'Ravenswing'
Arctotis 'Torch Purple'
Begonia 'Paul Hernandez'
Boronia heterophylla
Campanula portenschlagiana
Canna 'Black Knight'
Carex testacea
Cestrum 'Newellii'
Chondropetalum tectorum
Clerondendrum bungei
Colocasia esculenta 'Fontanesii'
Cornus stolonifera 'Isanti'
Crinum asiaticum
Cuphea hyssopifolia 'Allyson
  Purple', 'Lavender'
Dianella tasmanica
Dietes 'Orange Drop'
Festuca muelleri 'Mueller's Fescue'
Fuchsia procumbens
Fuchsia thymifolia 'Variegata'
Gaura lindheimeri 'Siskiyou Pink'
Geranium maderense
Hebe 'Amy', 'McKeanii'
Heliotropium arborescens
Helleborus argutifolius
Hydrangea macrophylla
  'Mariesii', 'Veitchii'
Ixia flexuosa
Loropetalum chinense 'Plum
  Delight', 'Razzleberri'
Nandina domestica 'Gulfstream'
Osmanthus heterophyllus 'Goshiki'
Parahebe linifolia
Pelargonium sidoides
Phormium tenax 'Bronze Baby'
Rosa 'Iceberg', 'Trumpeter'
Rumex sanguineus
Russelia equisetiformis

Russelia equisetiformis 'Aurea'
Salix irrorata
Verbena × hybrida 'Tapien Blue'
Veronica peduncularis
  'Georgia Blue'

AREA 4

Abelia × grandiflora 'Aurea'
Acorus gramineus 'Ogon',
  'Variegatus'
Agapanthus 'Streaks', 'Tinker Bell'
Asteriscus sericeus
Begonia 'Richmondensis'
Campanula gargarica
  'Dickson's Gold'
Canna 'Pretoria'
Carex elata 'Aurea'
Carex testacea
Choisya ternata 'Sundance'
Coleonema pulchrum
  'Golden Sunset'
Coprosma repens 'Jim Duggan',
  'Marble Queen'
Cordyline australis 'Albertii'
Cornus alba 'Spaethii'
Cornus stolonifera 'Flaverimea'
Cuphea hyssopifolia 'Aurea'
Euphorbia dulcis 'Chameleon'
Euphorbia tirucallii 'Sticks of Fire'
Felicia amelloides 'Variegata'
Geranium maderense
Heliotropium arborescens
Ixia maculata
Libertia peregrinans
Lilium 'Enchantment'
Lysimachia nummularia 'Aurea'
Nicotiana 'Lime Green'
Origanum 'Betty Rollins'
Pelargonium graveolens
  'Lady Plymouth'
Pelargonium × hortorum
  'Vancouver Centennial'
Phormium 'Apricot Queen',
  'Guardsman', 'Jack Spratt',
  'Surfer'
Phormium cookianum
  'Maori Queen'
Phormium tenax 'Yellow Wave'
Russelia equisetiformis
Salix 'Flame'
Sedum confusum
Silene uniflora 'Druett's Variety'
Solenostemon scutellarioides
  'Pineapple'
Spiraea japonica 'Gold Flame'
Tanacetum parthenium 'Aureum'
Thymus 'Transparent Yellow'
Thymus × citriodorus 'Lime'
Trifolium pratense 'Susan Smith'
Tropaeolum majus

AREA 5

Calylophus drummondianus
Campanula gargarica
  'Dickson's Gold'
Dymondia margaretae
Equisetum scirpoides
Limonium psilocladium
Origanum × majoricum
  'Well Sweep'
Origanum vulgare 'Jim Best'
Sedum 'Flori'
Thymus serpyllum 'Elfin'

AREA 6

Acalypha wilkesiana 'Haleakala'
Ajuga reptans 'Catlin's Giant'
Angelica stricta 'Purpurea'
Anthriscus sylvestris 'Ravenswing'
Armeria maritima 'Rubrifolia'
Aster lateriflorus 'Lady in Black'
Berberis vulgaris 'Purple Cloak'
Canna 'Intrigue', 'Phaison',
  'Red Stripe'
Cordyline australis 'Sundance'
Cornus stolonifera 'Isanti'
Crinum asiaticum
Dahlia 'Fascination',
  'Rip City', 'Ripples'
Fuchsia triphylla
  'Gartenmeister Bonstedt'
Haloragis erectus
  'Wellington Bronze'
Hemerocallis 'Red Tet'
Iris 'Sapphire Beauty'
Libertia peregrinans
Loropetalum chinense
  'Plum Delight'
Lysimachia ciliata 'Purpurea'
Nandina domestica 'Longden
  Pearl', 'Moyer's Red'
Papaver rhoeas
Rosa 'Meidiland Red'
Trifolium repens 'Atropurpureum'
Tulipa 'Negrita','Shirley'
Uncinia uncinata
Viola tricolor 'Prince Henry'

AREA 7

Astelia chathamica 'Silver Spear'
Astelia nivicola 'Red Gem'
Athanasia acerosa
Babiana 'Rubrocyanea'
Bauhinia corymbosa
Bracteantha bracteata
  'Soft Yellow'
Calamintha grandiflora
  'Variegata'
Catananche caerulea 'Bicolor'

Cercis canadensis 'Silver Cloud'
Clematis tangutica
Dahlia 'Gitts Attention',
  'Tanjoh', 'Worton's Blue Streak'
Deschampsia cespitosa
  'Northern Lights'
Dianella tasmanica 'Blushy'
Diascia 'Ice Cracker'
Echium vulgare 'Blue Bedder'
Eryngium 'Sapphire Blue'
Eryngium maritimum
Eryngium variifolium
Euphorbia cotinifolia
Euphorbia rigida
Euphorbia tirucallii 'Sticks of Fire'
Geranium harveyi
Glaucium flavum
Helleborus argutifolius
  'Janet Starnes'
Iris 'White Wedgewood'
Ixia viridiflora
Lavandula × heterophylla
  'Goodwin Creek'
Lavandula × intermedia
  'Walbertons's Silver Edge'
Leucanthemum × superbum
  'Esther Read'
Linaria purpurea 'Natalie'
Lobelia erinus 'Crystal Palace'
Lychnis coronaria
Nectaroscordum siculum
Nemesia 'Innocence'
Oenanthe japonica 'Flamingo'
Origanum × majoricum 'Well Sweep'
Oxalis 'Garnet'
Papaver somniferum 'Lavender
  Breadseed', 'White Peony'
Pelargonium sidoides
Portulacaria afra 'Variegata'
Rhodanthemum hosmariense
Rosa 'Dublin Bay', 'Sea Foam'
Rosa wichurana 'Variegata'
Ruta graveolens 'Variegata'
Salix irrorata
Salvia chamaedryoides
Santolina chamaecyparissus
  'Lemon Queen'
Silene uniflora 'Druett's Variety'
Solanum jasminoides 'Album'
Strobilanthes isophyllus
Tanacetum ptarmiciflorum
Verbascum chaixii 'Album'
Vitis vinifera 'Purpurea'

AREA 8

Abelia × grandiflora 'Confetti'
Achillea millefolium 'Red Beauty'
Agapanthus 'Elaine'
Agrostemma githago 'Milas'
Alstroemeria 'Rachel'

Index of Scientific and Common Names

Page numbers in **boldface** refer to main entries; those in *italics* refer to illustrations. Garden sections are indicated in square brackets after each entry.

Cover: *Helenium autumnale* 'Moerheim Beauty'
Endpapers: *Phormium* 'Tiny Tim'
p. iv: *Anigozanthus flavidus* 'Bush Sunset'
p. vi: *Thalictrum delavayi* 'Hewitt's Double'
pp. xii–xiii: Area 8 of the Bowl Garden
p. 2: *Brugmansia suaveolens* 'Charles Grimaldi'
p. 6: "Tapestry Effect" in the Bowl Garden
p. 24: Bowl Garden with the Azalea Pool
p. 34: *Chondropetalum tectorum*
p. 35 (top): *Cordyline australis* 'Albertii'
p. 35 (bottom): *Cordyline australis* 'Sundance'
p. 36: *Coprosma repens* 'Jim Duggan'
p. 37: *Fallopia japonica* 'Variegata'
p. 38 (top): *Catananche caerulea* 'Bicolor'
p. 38 (bottom): *Acalypha wilkesiana* 'Haleakala'
p. 39: *Eryngium* 'Sapphire Blue'
p. 40 (top): *Stigmaphyllon ciliatum*
p. 40 (bottom): *Papaver somniferum* 'Lavender Breadseed'
p. 41: *Anigozanthus flavidus* 'Bush Sunset'
p. 42: *Dianella tasmanica*
p. 43: *Rosa* 'Sea Foam'
pp. 130–31: *Ipomoea lobata*